Overcoming Common Problems

Overcoming Worry and Anxiety

DR JERRY KENNARD

First published in Great Britain in 2014

Sheldon Press
36 Causton Street
London SW1P 4ST
www.sheldonpress.co.uk

British Library Cataloguing-in-Publication Data
A catalogue record for this book is available from the British Library

ISBN 978–1–84709–322–6
eBook ISBN 978–1–84709–323–3

Typeset by Caroline Waldron, Wirral, Cheshire
First printed in Great Britain by Ashford Colour Press
Subsequently digitally reprinted in Great Britain

eBook by Fakenham Photosetting Ltd, Fakenham, Norfolk NR21 8NN

Produced on paper from sustainable forests

Dr Jerry Kennard is a chartered psychologist and associate fellow of the British Psychological Society. He is an established health blogger and author of self-help books. He currently contributes regular blogs to Remedy Health Media and was formerly the men's health guide to About.com.

Dr Kennard began his career in mental health and worked in a variety of settings. Two decades later he moved into higher education, where he subsequently headed a university department of psychology. He lives close to the city of York in the UK. Jerry can be contacted via his website <www.jerrykennard.net>.

Overcoming Common Problems Series

Selected titles

A full list of titles is available from Sheldon Press,
36 Causton Street, London SW1P 4ST and on our website at
www.sheldonpress.co.uk

Breast Cancer: Your treatment choices
Dr Terry Priestman

Chronic Fatigue Syndrome: What you need to know about CFS/ME
Dr Megan A. Arroll

Cider Vinegar
Margaret Hills

Coping Successfully with Chronic Illness: Your healing plan
Neville Shone

Coping Successfully with Shyness
Margaret Oakes, Professor Robert Bor and Dr Carina Eriksen

Coping with Difficult Families
Dr Jane McGregor and Tim McGregor

Coping with Epilepsy
Dr Pamela Crawford and Fiona Marshall

Coping with Guilt
Dr Windy Dryden

Coping with Liver Disease
Mark Greener

Coping with Memory Problems
Dr Sallie Baxendale

Coping with Obsessive Compulsive Disorder
Professor Kevin Gournay, Rachel Piper and Professor Paul Rogers

Coping with Schizophrenia
Professor Kevin Gournay and Debbie Robson

Coping with Thyroid Disease
Mark Greener

Depressive Illness: The curse of the strong
Dr Tim Cantopher

The Diabetes Healing Diet
Mark Greener and Christine Craggs-Hinton

The Empathy Trap: Understanding antisocial personalities
Dr Jane McGregor and Tim McGregor

Epilepsy: Complementary and alternative treatments
Dr Sallie Baxendale

Fibromyalgia: Your treatment guide
Christine Craggs-Hinton

Hay Fever: How to beat it
Dr Paul Carson

The Heart Attack Survival Guide
Mark Greener

Helping Elderly Relatives
Jill Eckersley

The Holistic Health Handbook
Mark Greener

How to Eat Well When You Have Cancer
Jane Freeman

How to Stop Worrying
Dr Frank Tallis

The Irritable Bowel Diet Book
Rosemary Nicol

Living with Complicated Grief
Professor Craig A. White

Living with IBS
Nuno Ferreira and David T. Gillanders

Making Sense of Trauma: How to tell your story
Dr Nigel C. Hunt and Dr Sue McHale

Overcoming Fear: With mindfulness
Deborah Ward

Overcoming Loneliness
Alice Muir

Overcoming Stress
Professor Robert Bor, Dr Carina Eriksen and Dr Sara Chaudry

Overcoming Worry and Anxiety
Dr Jerry Kennard

Physical Intelligence: How to take charge of your weight
Dr Tom Smith

The Self-Esteem Journal
Alison Waines

Ten Steps to Positive Living
Dr Windy Dryden

Transforming Eight Deadly Emotions into Healthy Ones
Dr Windy Dryden

Treating Arthritis: The drug-free way
Margaret Hills and Christine Horner

Treating Arthritis: The supplements guide
Julia Davies

Understanding Yourself and Others: Practical ideas from the world of coaching
Bob Thomson

When Someone You Love Has Depression: A handbook for family and friends
Barbara Baker

Contents

About this book   vii

1   Worry, anxiety, stress and fear   1

2   Mind and body   16

3   Symptoms and conditions   23

4   Work and lifestyle   40

5   Medical and related anxieties   51

6   Thinking about therapy   55

7   Guided and supportive therapies   59

8   Self-help and remedies   69

9   Cultivating calm and confidence   89

10 Assertion   96

11 Moving forwards   103

Useful addresses   105

References   107

Index   109

Contents

About this book

The lived experience of worry and anxiety is often complex, embarrassing and hard to explain. For information and help, people frequently turn to books like this. So what about this book? Well, I've spent many years and more than one occupation dealing with issues of worry, anxiety and stress. I've listened to those who suffer with them and I've helped to treat them. I've also written extensively about anxiety disorders and answered questions via blogs, emails and face-to-face interactions. These experiences have taught me that people want answers to questions in ways I might consider disorganized or possibly even unhelpful, but it's what's on *their* mind that counts and it's what *they* would like answering that matters.

This book will make plain the complexities involved in the mechanisms of worry and anxiety. It will offer you insights and advice about treatment and self-help options in ways that are practicable and easy to follow. I've also included several links to YouTube videos that help expand on topics I've covered. And as so much of the content has been guided by your questions and concerns, I hope *you* will find the material both interesting and helpful.

Jerry Kennard

1

Worry, anxiety, stress and fear

Illness and responsibilities

If we get into conversation about our worries and the uncomfortable sensations they arouse we can be pretty certain the person listening can sympathize – to a greater or lesser extent – with our experiences. This is because worry and anxiety are universal. We are born with anxiety and without it we would have no internal mechanism to monitor and respond to real or perceived threats.

Anxiety is both normal and necessary, but beyond this are situations and circumstances that evoke high levels of worry and anxiety in the face of proportionately low levels of threat. It is these more extreme levels of anxiety that provoke a wide variety of questions and explanations.

The focus of this book is to explore some of the features of high and often persistent levels of worry and anxiety. In doing so, I attempt to answer your questions about the nature of the beast before considering ways we might reduce its worst effects.

So what's the difference between worry and anxiety? Well, they are related of course, but technically worry refers to the thought processes that result in anxiety. Thus worry precedes anxiety, which is an important distinction when it comes to managing worry. The way we *think* leads to the feelings and emotions we describe as anxiety. As the book progresses you will see how certain therapeutic approaches target the way we think and behave in order to reduce anxiety.

Before I press on, a word of caution. Too much focus on the symptoms of anxiety can distort perceptions. Feeling anxious, even for a protracted period of time, may be uncomfortable but it is not necessarily a sign of psychological illness. We have to account for the context in which symptoms occur before being tempted to label ourselves, or others, as having some kind of anxiety disorder.

There is also a basic danger in medicalizing the effect of a problem rather than its cause, which is always something of a dilemma with conventional treatment methods. Giving people pills for anxiety because, for example, we can't address the poverty and lifestyle issues that cause their symptoms is a case in point. Even so, over the past few years there has been a considerable shift in the way medicine operates (no pun intended). People in my own 50-plus generation were pretty well indoctrinated into the idea that sickness belonged to medicine – you gave yourself over to the doctors and followed their orders. These days the picture is changing and many of our doctor–patient interactions are in the form of information-sharing and agreeing strategies and treatments. Many of these, you may be surprised to learn, are within our own gift and require no medication.

Doctor, doctor . . .

The medical profession freely acknowledges that, in some areas at least, what they can offer has limitations. This has given rise to more collective forms of therapy in which doctors, other health professionals and sometimes people once considered outside of therapy can provide a more comprehensive range of interventions.

Despite this, many people still place ultimate faith in medicine to provide them with an answer, preferably in the form of a cure. It isn't easy to be told your faith in medicine is sometimes misplaced. Having your doctor point out, often in the kindest way, that you have to take some responsibility for your anxiety is tough. To be asked to take control of something you feel powerless over may even feel like an act of betrayal. You may feel your symptoms have been misunderstood or you may begin to question the competence of the doctor. Such issues are understandable in the context of beliefs you may hold about medicine but they also reveal a pattern of thinking that is typical of anxiety and therefore something only you can change.

Many people with anxiety come to rely on doctors to tell them, sometimes repeatedly, that nothing is physically wrong with them. Here are people who monitor any minor change in physical symptoms. They worry because they feel sick, nauseous, dizzy and more, and somewhere in the back of their minds is the hope and belief this new symptom will be enough for their doctor to piece the puzzle together and tell them what's really wrong. So to be told that these physical symptoms actually result from anxiety places them in a situation where to get relief from symptoms they must treat their anxiety.

To be asked to shoulder some responsibility for your worry and anxiety is not the same as being told to go away. It is merely the first and most important step in appreciating that your own thoughts and actions have a profound effect on your well-being.

The types of people who worry and suffer with anxiety vary greatly, but we know that relief can and will come from owning and mastering certain coping skills. Medication may also be useful, but a complex job often requires more than one tool!

Now let's dig a little deeper into the nature of worry and anxiety, how it applies to us and what we can do about it.

Anxiety and stress

As worry is to anxiety, so is there a relationship between anxiety and stress. It's worth taking a moment to consider the issues.

Anxiety is an emotional sensation. It's the uneasy and apprehensive feeling we get when we're emotionally or physically threatened.

Stress is often thought of as a development of situations that make us feel angry, irritated or frustrated. But stress is also a response to things like viruses, heat, cold, hunger and thirst. Stress is the way the body reacts to situations in which a decision is needed, or an action, threat or some imbalance to its normal functioning occurs. It is a protective mechanism usually, but if constantly triggered it becomes a health issue.

Everyone knows what a stressful day feels like. It leaves you depleted, tired and often with a headache. During stress your body reacts in a certain way – it pushes out adrenaline and various stress hormones and makes your heart work faster. This is excellent for situations in the short term but less good over long periods of time.

Any job is stressful in which the meeting of deadlines is essential or your performance is on display and being judged by others.

Even more stressful is having to deal with disgruntled people, take on extra work or having a boss you can't get on with. The role of long-term caregiver is also stressful, often because of the social isolation, repetitive demands and sleep disruptions that come with it. Despite all this, you may not feel *anxious*.

Where confusion arises, I think, is that we often talk about stress and anxiety as if they are one and the same thing, much in the way we refer to worry and anxiety. Another reason may be that people often only acknowledge they are stressed once they experience symptoms of acute anxiety. They find they can't concentrate as well as they used to, sleep may become disrupted and moods more tetchy and irritable. In some situations they may develop anxiety or panic attacks.

Anxiety and stress follow parallel paths. Independently of each other they can present a variety of health issues yet sometimes their paths cross and coincide. As anxiety often develops from stress it is possible to reduce anxiety by reducing stress. The good news is that a number of tried, tested and effective methods exist that allow us all to tackle either our anxiety, our stress or both.

Why do we worry?

We've all heard it and we've all said it: 'Don't worry – it'll all work out.' The sentiment is well intentioned but how accurate or useful is it? We often describe our less appealing emotions as negative. Grief, depression, anxiety and worry all fall into this category but it doesn't mean they are without purpose.

One of the key characteristics of worry is the way concerns just turn over and over in the mind, often with no apparent purpose or resolution. Apart from our insides being chewed up, the effect of worry can be sleepless nights, distraction from other activities and a focus on negative rather than positive outcomes. It is hardly surprising, then, that worry is universally regarded as a negative emotion.

You're probably reading this book because you see yourself as a person who worries, and perhaps this in itself worries you. It's much more common than you might think, but to reduce the negative effects of worrying I think it's helpful to gain some insight into how our own worry processes operate.

I'd like you to spend a few moments thinking about the issues that trigger your own worrying. Are they family related? Maybe they are things you read or see on television. Perhaps they are work issues. Of course they could be all or none of these things.

The chances are that your list includes one or more issues from finances, health issues, personal relationships and/or work. I can certainly relate to every one of these, and this is because they are among the most common worries, whether or not you consider yourself a worrier. But if we contrast this with, say, people with a generalized anxiety disorder (GAD), we begin to see a difference between what's normal and what isn't. People with GAD tend to focus a lot more on illness and poor health – their own and others'. They also tend to think that no other person worries the way they worry and that their worry is fully out of control, a process the psychologist Adrian Wells describes as meta-worry.

An obvious question is why we are burdened with worry. Jeremy Coplan, a professor of psychiatry, believes there is an evolutionary link between worry and intelligence. According to Coplan there is a correlation between high IQ and worry. Previous studies have also noted that excessive worry tends to exist in people with higher and lower intelligence and less so in people of average intelligence. Coplan's view is that this association would have had certain evolutionary benefits. Basically, high IQ worriers would be more likely to weigh up the potential risks of situations and take fewer chances, thus increasing their likelihood of survival. Those who suffer with anxiety and have lower intelligence often achieve less success in life and, in a complex modern world, may have less resilience and fewer personal coping strategies upon which to call.

But does this mean that worrying can actually be good for us today? It seems there's a balance to be struck. The negative side of excessive worry is that it can be emotionally debilitating. There is also a physical toll, which can include a higher heart rate and sinus arrhythmia – a naturally occurring variation in heart rate during a breathing cycle. Chronic worrying can also trigger the stress response, which is known to have a number of health implications.

On the plus side there is always the possibility that it is our concerns over the consequences of certain activities that keep us safe and healthy. The motivation for many smokers to quit is based around their concerns over cancer, heart problems and general health issues. The same might be said for diet, voluntary screening, breast self-examination and so on. Clearly there is a dividing line between health concerns and chronic worrying, but they are underpinned by the same basic mechanisms. The old saying 'ignorance is bliss' may be true up to a point, but you mustn't view your capacity to worry as entirely without use or merit.

This may be a good time for you to explore your own beliefs about worrying and whether you regard your own worrying as negative, positive or a mixture of the two. An example of negative beliefs is that your worrying makes you ill, that it might be getting worse and that you're losing control. By contrast, positive beliefs might be that your worrying keeps you focused, helps you to identify potential problems before they occur and is necessary to keep you sharp and on top of things.

Whether you consider your worrying as negative, positive or both, the fact remains that it is still worry. People who worry about worrying often adopt what is known as a 'what if' style of thinking. As the worry progresses it becomes more negative in nature. Here's an example:

> Tom is a well-regarded science teacher with ten years' experience under his belt. The train on which he commutes to and from work is often stuffy and crowded, and this evening someone kept sniffing and sneezing. A string of worrying thoughts begins to unfold in Tom's mind: 'What if I catch a cold, or flu?' he thinks. 'I'll have to take time off work.'

Because he's a worrier, Tom's imagination leads him along a path that becomes more catastrophic in nature. Thus 'I could lose my chances of a promotion' might build to a crescendo in 'I could even lose my job.'

Tom's story is a fiction but it represents a form of extreme and uncontrollable worry that won't diminish. Persistent worrying like this tells us that Tom's mood is increasingly negative, and he believes his problems will worsen and can't be solved. Negative thinking as a feature of worry is something I'll address a little later.

It's also clear that Tom's worry is pointless, but it does demonstrate two common characteristics of worry: first, it is unimportant; second, the outcomes conjured up are unlikely. Tom may or may not catch a cold, but how important is that? Also, how realistic are his thoughts about losing his job? And how did Tom get to such a point where he even thinks like this?

Unlocking anxiety

It's no understatement to say that most people who experience clinical levels of anxiety or depression have had difficulties in their early lives. It doesn't necessarily mean one leads to the other, and it doesn't preclude those with a secure upbringing from having these problems, but the association is noticeable, as is the way early life experiences often occupy a central position in affected people's memories.

Psychologists continue to gain insights into both the nature and effects of worry and anxiety. We now recognize that childhood disorders can cast long shadows and extend into adulthood. We also know from research following people from birth into adulthood that most young adults with a mental-health problem had diagnosable problems much earlier in life. How early these problems start and the mechanisms that link childhood adversity and trauma to adult life are more speculative matters. So-called adult disorders may have been set in motion during pre- and/or postnatal stages of development, yet for the most part our system of diagnosis places most weight on current symptoms, while acknowledging that there may be some 'history'.

One of the most researched areas in child–parent relationships is around attachment and/or separation. The unique bond between a mother and her infant is so universal that it has allowed scientists to study it in everything from rats to primates – the results are remarkably similar to humans. From some of these animal studies we know that baby rats separated from their mothers show a higher stress response rate later in life. We know that monkeys separated at birth from their mothers can develop strong bonds with others in a similar situation but remain more anxious and more vulnerable to anxiety and depression later in life.

The psychiatrist and psychoanalyst John Bowlby identified the huge importance of the parent–child relationship in the early years of life and how this goes on to influence future outcomes.

Later developments in the field by Allan Schore showed how Bowlby's ideas could be proved biologically. Schore made the case that the development of an area of the brain known as the prefrontal cortex depends on a positive emotional experience between parent and child.

The prefrontal cortex is involved with the control of pleasure, pain, anger, panic and other emotions and urges. Unlike other organs, which develop automatically, this part of the brain appears to be strongly affected by anxiety and depression. In a healthy nurturing relationship it will grow and form connections with other areas of the brain, but where this is lacking the prefrontal cortex will not develop fully. Some studies of neglected babies (such as Eluvathingal et al., 2006) reveal that they have smaller prefrontal cortexes than normal.

Parenting style and childhood anxiety

This brings us rather neatly to the question of what makes a good parent. Some people feel they're born for the task but for most others it feels more like a case of trial and error. Every new generation of parents lives in a world that is quite different in many ways from that experienced by their parents.

Not so long ago people looked to outside experts for guidance on how best to raise children. Dr Benjamin Spock is the most notable example. Spock sold over 50 million copies of his book *Baby and Child Care* and became a legend in his own lifetime. It's easy to forget quite how much Spock's ideas changed the way people viewed parenting. He gave parents permission to be their own experts in the way they nurtured and brought up their children. Later in his life Spock would be accused by some of fostering a new generation of spoiled and self-centred children.

Today psychologists talk about parenting styles and how these have a bearing on the development of the child. These styles can be classified into three broad types:

1 Permissive parenting – characterized by a lack of boundary-setting or of the requirement that behaviour be appropriately mature.

2 Authoritarian parenting – emotionally cold, inflexible and frequently severe in dealing with perceived errors or bad behaviour.

3 Authoritative parenting – sets clear boundaries but is also responsive to needs, supportive and assumes high standards of behaviour (see Baumrind, 1991).

In relation to the development of anxiety in children, the spotlight has fallen on the effect of parenting styles. The Harvard psychologists Jerome Kagan and Doreen Arcus, well-known researchers in the field of child development, say that 'parents' actions affect the probability of anxiety disorder in the child'. Kagan states that the parents in their study are all middle class and loving, but within that context:

two philosophies are represented. One is, 'I have a sensitive child that I must protect from stress.' So this parent, finding the child playing with rubbish tends not to set limits with a firm 'Don't do that,' but distracts the child. As a result, the child does not get the opportunity to extinguish the fear response.

Kagan contrasts this with the authoritative parent who has no difficulty in lifting the child's hands out of the trash and saying 'No. No rubbish', in which a clear boundary is established.

Can we demonstrate a relationship between this and later adult disorders? Possibly. Michael Liebowitz, the head of Columbia University's unit for panic disorders, told a meeting of the American Psychiatric Association that he finds that unusually high proportions of panic patients say they had overprotective parenting in childhood.

Research to emerge from parenting styles shows a remarkably consistent pattern in the way children develop. For example, children whose parents are authoritative rate themselves – and are rated by objective measures – as more socially and instrumentally competent. Children and adolescents from authoritarian families tend to perform moderately well in school and avoid problem behaviour but have poorer social skills, lower self-esteem and higher levels of depression. Children and adolescents from indulgent homes are more likely to be involved in problem behaviour and perform less well in school, but they have higher self-esteem, better social skills and lower levels of depression.

One of the main reasons people react so strongly to stressful events is that negative emotions are stored as memories in the unconscious mind. These implicit or embedded memories are located in an almond-shaped area of the brain known as the amygdala, which is sometimes thought of as the fear centre of the brain. Conditions such as anxiety, autism, depression, post-traumatic stress disorder (PTSD) and phobias are all suspected of being linked to abnormal functioning of the amygdala.

The fact that we can retrieve negative memories so rapidly is part of the problem. What originally evolved as a mechanism to help remind and protect us against genuine threats seems to be oversensitive in some people, which results in a strong reaction to situations perceived as threatening. If malign memories are stored during childhood they can continue to affect us as adults, even though as adults we may not be conscious of them. Each time stressful experiences are encountered there is an amplification of negative memories, which can dictate our responses.

This in part explains why people who suffer with anxiety find the situation so frustrating. At one level they are entirely aware that their worries and their emotional and behavioural reactions are way out of proportion to their situation, yet at another level they feel incapable of more adaptive responses. This is the problem of implicit memories – they can affect both our moods and thoughts in ways that are irrational, and we have no way of knowing why.

Some of the so-called talking therapies try to work with the person to access and redevelop implicit memories. This way, the underlying causes of anxiety and depression can be uncovered and coping strategies developed to make them more tolerable.

As a worrier you will already be applying your own coping strategies, but because they are not very effective you continue to worry. Consider for a moment the times you have avoided something because you've worried about the outcome.

Are you perhaps attuned to thinking: 'I won't manage it', 'People will see through me' or 'I'll show myself up and fail'? Avoidance is certainly one way of coping, but it severely restricts opportunities and feeds the worries you already experience.

Now think about the times you have attempted some kind of thought control such as: 'I must stop myself thinking like this.' It's called thought suppression and it's, well, useless. I'll prove it:

Try *not* to think about a monkey.

Maybe you've tried reasoning with your own thoughts – for example: 'It's pointless worrying, there's nothing I can do about it.' That's true, yet still you worry. Why? Because in your head there's still that niggling doubt, that need for an answer and some certainty.

Let's recap. So far I've outlined the importance of our beliefs in terms of how these influence worrying. I've mentioned the various triggers and the ways we cope with worry and its associated anxiety. You may also have noticed my emphasis on negative thinking – this is because negative thinking underpins worry.

Neutralizing negative thinking

Negative thinking is a difficult thing to shake off. Some of the beliefs that underpin the thoughts have been developed and refined from a very young age and run so deep that you may find it hard to see them in yourself. Consider how the following might apply to you:

- You tend to make your mind up quickly about situations and have difficulty remaining neutral or considering other options.
- If you make a mistake you see it as a sign that you can't do anything right.
- You feel you know when another person thinks badly of you.
- You often feel embarrassed or responsible for the behaviour and actions of those around you.

These are just a few characteristics of negative thinking. It tends to nullify the fact that every situation has a number of possible interpretations. If your first thoughts tend to be negative, make yourself consider at least one possible alternative. Try it now:

Mary watches a car come to a screeching halt. Her immediate thought is: 'The idiot driver clearly wasn't concentrating.' What alternative, less negative evaluations might Mary have considered? Perhaps a pedestrian stepped out without looking, or a child has run out? Who knows – and that's the issue: we don't know about the situation until we establish the facts.

Neutralizing negative thinking isn't about replacing negative thinking with happy thoughts. It's more about accepting that you are thinking negatively and that this may have negative consequences. The same goes for catastrophic thinking. One way to tell if you're a catastrophic thinker is to listen to the language you use. For example:

- That's terrible and it's likely to get worse.
- It's utterly pointless – I don't know why I bother.
- Why hasn't he answered my text? What's wrong?
- This freckle looks big – skin cancer maybe?

So assuming the worst is a central feature of catastrophic thinking. Of course, it's all about context and the belief you have in the things you are saying, rather than the exaggerations we sometimes use in everyday conversation.

Neutralizing negative thinking for worry

I'd like to suggest two ways for you to neutralize your negative thinking. Both involve questions you must ask yourself. First, ask yourself: 'What's the likelihood of the things I am worrying about actually happening?' If the likelihood is low, then you're wasting your energies worrying. Second, ask yourself: 'How important is my worry?':

- What is the worst possible outcome if what I'm worrying about actually happens?
- Will I remember what I'm worrying about one week from now?
- Compared to other things I worry about, is this less worrying, about the same or more worrying?

If you struggle to answer questions like this, the chances are you have given the issue a significance it simply doesn't deserve. So what about those more significant and realistic worries? From time to time we all have them, but the trick is to learn how to problem-solve and then let them go. Here's what to do.

- If you believe you can do something about the worry, work out an action plan by considering the options.
- If you can do it now, fine; if not, let go of the worry by doing something more pleasurable or something that focuses your attention elsewhere.
- Don't indulge in checking, seeking reassurances or sitting by the telephone 'in case'.
- Don't avoid something if it needs to be dealt with. If, for example, you can't afford to pay a bill, worrying about it for days on end won't help. This is an example of a realistic worry that can be overcome by taking action.

Fears and uncertainties

During the years of the great depression it was Franklin D. Roosevelt who famously commented, 'The only thing we have to fear is fear itself.' The context and the timing of his remark were important. Fear is a universal emotion that varies in range, frequency and severity, and it can be helpful or unhelpful.

In normal circumstances, there tends to be a correspondence between levels of fear and threat – as the threat level increases, so does the fear. People with anxiety-related issues live fearful lives because one of the commonest problems they experience is an overestimation of threat, but in circumstances and situations that are usually commonplace and harmless. They also tend to predict the worst by overestimating their own fear response and underestimating their ability to cope.

According to Professor Stanley J. Rachman, a leading authority in anxiety and related disorders, similar patterns of behaviour are found in people who suffer from panic episodes. More often than not they will predict a panic attack when in fact none occurs. Despite clear evidence pointing to the unreliability of such predictions, the tendency to predict panic and the associated feelings of fear remain unchanged.

Fear is a combination of dread, physiological changes and a strong desire to avoid or escape. It is both a reaction and a motivating force. Fear may be rational, as in behaviour designed to avoid injury or trauma, or it may be irrational, as is the case in most phobias.

The overprediction of fear is closely linked to avoidance behaviour common in worry. You may have been trying out some of my previous suggestions for getting an edge over your worries, but one important area of worry we need to tackle is the thorny issue of uncertainty.

One of the reasons you worry is that you hate uncertainty. As I mentioned previously, it's that niggling doubt that keeps your worries alive. Worrying helps to reduce the sense of uncertainty by fuelling your imagination. You work out different scenarios and different outcomes in your mind, and this gives you a sense of predictability and control.

Unfortunately a *sense* of certainty is not the same as certainty. The fact that you might be able to say: 'I knew it. I told you so' on a very few occasions does not mean that your capacity to worry is synonymous with foresight. Worry will never change the outcome of something and neither will it make it any more certain.

Normal and generalized anxiety

It's a normal part of the human condition to worry about things. Some people seem more prone to it than others. So where is the dividing line between normal and generalized anxiety?

One of the biggest clues about our own anxiety state comes from comparing ourselves to others and receiving their feedback. We may, for example, notice that while everyone else seems relaxed, we are a bag of nerves. Perhaps others also tell us that we worry too much and too often over silly little things. This really is the nub of the matter with an anxiety condition I mentioned above known as generalized anxiety disorder. People with GAD worry about everything – constantly and excessively.

'What if?' questions are a real feature of GAD. These questions nearly always cluster around issues of health, family, money and work. In that regard they seem entirely normal but it is the duration and depth of concerns that distinguish GAD from what we might consider normal anxiety. These concerns also extend beyond the typical ones of everyday life and embrace issues of a global nature.

People with GAD are particularly sensitive to real or supposed feedback. For example, if someone at work is more efficient, or if there is the slightest hint she or he may have done something better, the alarm bells ring and thought processes quickly spin out of control, to a point where the person with GAD truly believes he or she is about to be fired. And a husband – people with GAD are usually women – who says he prefers one meal, one dress or one pair of shoes over another may be seen as preparing the ground for separation or divorce. The stress of living with GAD is such that while many people have little choice but to try to continue as normal a life as possible, some become too seriously affected.

At the point where normal functioning is affected, a diagnosis of GAD is likely to follow, especially if problems persist for several months. There may be symptoms of chronic worry, sleeping difficulties, a sense of dread and quite possibly a list of physical symptoms that the person has attributed to some life-threatening disease.

2

Mind and body

The link between anxiety and illness

Previously I cautioned against the danger of medicalizing anxiety when there may be any number of very practical causes that, if identified and acted upon, could provide a solution to symptoms. We also have to accept that some people appear prone to anxiety despite their circumstances appearing broadly similar to or sometimes better than those of others.

People who are vulnerable to anxiety tend to go through a particular set of routines when they enter a potentially intimidating situation. Rather like tuning a radio, they scan rapidly and broadly to identify possible threats. These potential threats are then tuned into and the volume is turned up in terms of their heightened state of arousal. The whole process involves a psychological interpretation of events but it also feeds into, and feeds off, changes in the body.

When something is appraised as potentially threatening, a part of the nervous system called the sympathetic nervous system kicks in. A rush of adrenaline and noradrenaline (see p. 20) floods the body. The heart rate quickens, sweating increases and pupils dilate. The body is designed around a simple fight-or-flight mechanism. Fight and flight are physical outlets, ideally used to dissipate stress when it occurs. In modern life our stress response is continually being triggered by such things as missing breakfast, late trains, barbed comments, prickly emails, lost keys, relationship issues – the list is endless. These examples don't lend themselves to fight or flight, so tension simply builds, with no obvious outlet. But these stress-provoking moments also trigger something called the hypothalamic–pituitary–adrenocortical (HPA) system. The HPA system produces a number of substances, the most important of which is the hormone cortisol. It is the combined effect of continued activation of the sympathetic nervous system and HPA activity that may have serious consequences for health.

Professor Jane Ogden, a health psychologist at the University of Surrey, states that prolonged production of adrenaline and noradrenaline can result in irregular heart beats, increased heart rate and blood pressure, increased risk of blood clot formation, fatty deposits and plaques, and suppression of the immune system. The body becomes more prone to infection and the risk of heart and kidney disease increases. Prolonged HPA activation also appears to decrease immune function and leads to damage in a region of the brain known as the hippocampus. Over time, psychological issues such as loss of memory, loss of concentration and psychiatric problems may appear.

Other important factors have to be accounted for when considering the link between stress and illness. Stress is often a trigger for additional activities that have a direct effect on health. The most obvious are smoking, drinking alcohol, changes to diet and less exercise.

Medical conditions

A variety of medical conditions are strongly associated with anxiety. Moreover any drug that affects the sympathetic nervous system is also a candidate for giving rise to anxiety symptoms (for example, asthma inhalers or nasal decongestants).

Hyperthyroidism, a condition in which the thyroid gland is overactive, can lead to anxiety. This is the most common of the endocrine diseases, occurring mainly in women between the ages of 20 and 40. Symptoms include a fine tremor, irritability, restlessness, insomnia, excitability, nervousness, sweating, palpitations and persistent fear and worry.

Mental-health symptoms are often some of the early signs of an underactive thyroid gland (hypothyroidism) – up to 12 per cent of cases report anxiety, poor memory, speech deficits and diminished learning capacity. Some estimates suggest that 30–40 per cent of people with hypothyroidism have an anxiety disorder. Once treatment commences, anxiety symptoms tend to subside anywhere from days to months later.

Chronic breathing disorders such as asthma or emphysema are often associated with anxiety. This is explained by the inability of the person to breathe effectively. Low blood sugar, not necessarily associated with diabetes, can also result in anxiety. This can occur in cases where the person is working hard and has overlooked a meal. Other medical conditions in which anxiety may be a feature include:

- obesity
- irritable bowel syndrome
- fibromyalgia
- super-ventricular arrhythmias
- ventricular arrhythmias
- migraine
- chronic obstructive pulmonary disease
- tumours of the adrenal gland.

The influence of brain chemicals

Many of our moods depend on our nervous system. Too much or too little of the chemicals in the nervous system – called neuro-transmitters – that speed things up or slow things down, and the whole thing can go out of kilter. The basis of many of our anxiety medications is to correct these imbalances. To form an appreciation of the issue, I shall outline four of these essential neurotrans-mitters – plus one other natural chemical – and the way they work.

Glutamate and GABA

Glutamate and gamma-aminobutyric acid (GABA) can be thought of as mainstay neurotransmitters. They slog away in high con-centrations within the brain, where glutamate is the throttle and GABA acts as the brake. Glutamate has an important role in learn-ing and memory, but too much of it can lead to agitation, impul-sive behaviour and even violence. GABA has the opposite effect. It increases our levels of tranquillity by inhibiting too much nerve activity. Some of the most frequently used drugs for anxiety aim to enhance the action of GABA.

Increasing your GABA levels naturally

Physical activity encourages the development of neurons in an area of the brain called the hippocampus, a portion of which is associated with processing emotions. Some of these new neurons are young and excitable but others are designed to release GABA. Elizabeth Gould, the director of the Gould Laboratory at Princeton University, has demonstrated that people who exercise regularly release more GABA during stressful situations. This in turn facilitates a more rapid recovery.

Mike Dow, a psychologist, makes various dietary suggestions, some of which are thought to increase GABA levels. Oolong tea, cherry tomatoes, kefir (a probiotic drink) and shrimp are some of the examples he offers, but they represent just part of a well-balanced diet that requires reduction in fatty, processed and sugary foods.

I mention exercise and diet because the evidence to date suggests that they influence mood greatly. The fact that a connection between mood and GABA has been established has resulted in some sections of the food-supplement industry making bold claims for the effects of their products. However, the supporting evidence is very thin, so do think carefully before parting with your cash for commercial GABA supplements.

Dopamine

Dopamine is our arousal and stimulation neurotransmitter. We associate dopamine with rewards because it controls our appetite for sex, eating, pleasure and even creative thinking. Too little dopamine can lead to depression but too much can lead to dependence on the agent doing the stimulating. Cocaine, for example, increases dopamine levels in the brain's reward circuit and, for a period, can produce intense pleasure. However, long-term use seems to result in neural degeneration from overproduction of dopamine.

Endorphins

Endorphins are both hormones and neurotransmitters and they can pack a punch. We have at least 20 different types of endorphin, some of which are more powerful than morphine. We release endorphins when we're under stress or in pain. The higher the level of endorphin, the less pain we feel and the more relaxed, even euphoric, we can become.

There is some speculation that a lack of endorphins could explain anxiety-related conditions such as obsessive–compulsive disorder (OCD) or even clinical depression. Endorphin deficiency disorder (EDS) may be genetic or acquired. The associated symptoms are very similar to clinical depression or bipolar disorder. Acquired EDS tends to be of shorter duration and can result from inadequate exercise, pain or emotional stress.

Increasing your endorphins naturally

Intense exercise can result in the so-called runner's high. That's one way to it, but if you'd prefer a less taxing alternative, try something like t'ai chi or meditation. A *light* intake of alcohol also stimulates endorphins, as do foods like chocolate and chilli peppers. Ultraviolet light also gets those endorphins moving, so get out and about during the day.

Noradrenaline

Noradrenaline (norepinephrine) is the main neurotransmitter of the sympathetic nervous system. We associate this with our fight-or-flight mechanism and moderation of other physical actions, such as heart rate and blood pressure. Too little noradrenaline and we become sleepy and lethargic; too much and our thoughts run away with us, we become twitchy and nervous, our hands and feet go cold and our blood pressure climbs.

Dynorphin

Dynorphin is not a neurotransmitter but I list it here as an example of a natural chemical known to influence anxiety. Dynorphin is produced in the brain and spinal cord. Chemically it has broadly similar properties to opiates such as opium and morphine, although studies suggest it is at least six times more powerful. Our bodies appear to produce different types of dynorphin, and these are involved in regulating emotion, motivation, our experience of pain and how we respond to stress.

Various studies show that the level of dynorphin in our bodies can have dramatically different effects. In some situations dynorphins can produce feelings of euphoria but in others can stimulate pain rather than relieving it. Some studies show that blocking dynorphin can reduce depression, yet high levels are linked with overeating, hyperthermia and resistance to cocaine addiction.

Andras Bilkei-Gorzo and colleagues from the Universities of Bonn and Berlin say that if the brain produces too little dynorphin, symptoms of anxiety will not subside. In one stress experiment, volunteers with lower gene activity for dynorphin were compared with those with higher activity. During the experiment volunteers wore computer glasses and were subjected variously to the appearance of blue and green squares. When green squares appeared an unpleasant stimulus to the back of the hand was applied using a laser. Stress reactions were observed by measuring increased sweat on the skin.

As part of the experiment, brain scans were taken. These revealed that volunteers in the low dynorphin group showed stress reactions for considerably longer than those in the high dynorphin group. The amygdala, an area of the brain that processes emotional content, was also shown to remain active for longer in the low dynorphin group.

The study suggests that *forgetting* anxiety is an active process that involves different parts of the brain. Volunteers in the low dynorphin group appeared to have less 'coupling' of these areas, which could explain why they retain the memory and anxiety associated with trauma for much longer.

The influence of context

It would be wrong to suggest that the primary cause of anxiety is some imbalance of brain chemicals. Let's take the example of generalized anxiety disorder, which I introduced in Chapter 1 (see p. 5).

Since her boyfriend walked out six months ago Jane, a 27-year-old with two young children, has been working at the local supermarket to make ends meet. She's visiting her doctor today because of headaches. During the consultation it emerges that Jane hasn't been sleeping well. When questioned it emerges that she actually feels anxious about all sorts of things for most of the time. Jane worries that her headaches and the tingling feeling in her hands means she is getting really sick. She tells the doctor that she feels jumpy and irritable, that she can't seem to focus and that she's preoccupied with thoughts that something terrible is about to happen to her or the children.

GAD is one of the most prevalent mental-health problems today. At any one time it affects around 4–5 per cent of the population. Of these, around 80 per cent have some accompanying condition, such as depression. As with so many other mental-health issues, questions surrounding its origins and development often hinge on nature versus nurture – that is, how influential genes or the environment are when it comes to understanding and treating such issues.

GAD is characterized by excessive and uncontrollable worry, usually but not necessarily related to areas of health, finances and minor matters that become blown out of proportion. Some people with GAD are simply unable to pin down a source of worry – a feature sometimes referred to as free-floating anxiety. Before a diagnosis of GAD is reached, a number of other symptoms, such as irritability, sleep difficulties, muscle tension and problems with concentration, also have to be evident for at least six months.

But to what extent is GAD the result of some internal psychological mechanism? The answer isn't clear but it does seem that context is important. Judith C. Baer and colleagues point out that studies of the poorest mothers show them as having the highest levels of GAD. And this, claim the authors, has nothing to do with some 'internal malfunction' so much as 'a reaction to severe environmental deficits'.

The danger in labelling a person with something like GAD is the assumption that the cause is some internal mental state. However, in situations as reported by Baer and colleagues, it becomes clear that context is important. GAD can and does respond to treatment, but if the cause is poverty, it stands to reason that 'financial help and concrete services' are likely to be more appropriate.

Anxiety disorders are also associated with a number of physical conditions linked to poor quality of life and disability. GAD is recognized as a condition that carries a high cost in personal suffering. Suicidal thoughts and suicide attempts significantly increase, especially in women, when GAD is accompanied by depression.

3

Symptoms and conditions

Becky is far from confident. Ever since she can remember she has lived with feelings of tension and insecurity. It's often worse at night as she thinks about the following day, what is involved and whether she will cope. She becomes more apprehensive and calculates ways to avoid the more worrying situations. As the tension increases she begins to feel nauseous. Her heart pounds, her stomach knots up and she begins to sweat.

Physical signs of anxiety

Our bodies prefer to exist in a state of balance. Even so, they are adapted to respond to the demands required of them, before returning to a state of balance. For this state of self-regulation to occur we have bodily mechanisms that speed us up and slow us down. When the sympathetic nervous system – see Chapter 2 – kicks in we are in fight-or-flight mode and ready for action. When the *para*sympathetic nervous system dominates we are in a state of 'rest and digest' – our heart rate slows, intestinal and gland activity increase and we conserve energy.

Our fight-or-flight mechanism enables us to cope with threats; it represents our survival instinct. When a threat is sensed, the fear centre in the brain – the amygdala – starts a chain reaction that results in the release of the stress hormones adrenaline, noradrenaline and cortisol. These hormones make the heart beat faster, divert blood to muscles and increase levels of glucose in the blood to act as an energy reserve. The air passages dilate to allow more oxygen to be taken in and digestion slows as energy is diverted for other needs.

Unfortunately our fight-or-flight capabilities are somewhat lessened in modern living. Instead we find ourselves subjected to all the stressors that activate the sympathetic nervous system but with outlets that rarely involve fight or flight. When the sympathetic nervous system kicks in it can leave us with some fairly unpleasant physical sensations to deal with, including:

- palpitations and chest pains
- sweating
- dizziness
- dry mouth
- trembling
- tingling
- muscle tension and stomach cramps
- feeling faint and sometimes feelings of unreality
- nausea
- urge to urinate
- tightness in the throat and difficulty swallowing.

Anxiety sometimes extends to everyday living and the very dramatic sensations associated with fight or flight are much less pronounced. Here's an example from my own experience.

> I've always had a dislike of heights – actually it's more a concern about falling from them as I can sit quite happily on an aircraft at 35,000 feet. However, put me on something 35 feet above the ground with no barrier and I begin to feel uncomfortable. It's a situation that on a day-to-day level hardly affects me at all but it can get awkward.
>
> When my family first moved to York we did the tourist trail. This included walking the famous city walls, which occasionally lack any kind of barrier and can be a little narrow underfoot. To my continued embarrassment I remember meeting a party of elderly people walking in the opposite direction. To avoid the side with no barrier I pinned myself to the wall, which meant they had to work around me. I can't remember how much of a drop it was but it won't have been much. But to me – the person who gets dizzy on a thick carpet – it really didn't matter because I was too into avoidance to notice!
>
> My level of discomfort is by no means off the scale. I'm more at the prefer-not-to-if-I-don't-have-to level, and I've certainly been in other 'barrier-less' situations and coped, despite the discomfort. Basically I'm largely able to ignore it and because it doesn't intrude on my daily living, that's how I continue to rationalize it.

I offer this as an example precisely because it isn't my intention to approach this book from a superior position. Like you, I worry about things and I sometimes feel anxious – that is, I'm normal. Like you I have bills to pay, family issues and concerns to contend with, and I sometimes come across situations and people that make me feel uncomfortable. But I've also learned to recognize the signs, the patterns of thought, the behaviours and emotions associated with my discomfort and – importantly – learned what to do about it.

How do we respond to stress?

Well, I've said it's down to fight or flight, but does this explanation work as well for women as it seems to for men? Not necessarily, according to research conducted over the past decade. Before I address this it might be helpful to provide some perspective and take a step back in time.

In the 1920s Walter Cannon first described the 'acute stress response' and the way our nervous system and hormones respond when we perceive a state of threat. What this boils down to is this: the greater our perception of threat, the more intense and prolonged our physical reaction to it will be. In order to dispel the threat, we're left with two basic choices: deal with it (fight) or get away from it (flight).

Since then our understanding of the stress response has become more refined, but it is still based largely on the basic principle of fight or flight. A question asked more recently is how well these early principles tally with what we know about women.

Professor Shelley Taylor and colleagues decided to look at things differently. From their perspective, women are considered less likely to benefit from fight or flight, especially if they have babies or young children. They also reasoned that females of different species tend to form tight, stable alliances, which might suggest a greater need to seek out supportive relationships. Having set the scene, the team embarked on a programme of research that examined diverse cultures as well as studies on everything from rats to primates. What transpired has developed into the first new model of stress for decades.

The 'tend-and-befriend' model is not an alternative to fight or flight. Indeed the authors point out that the initial shock response in terms of hormonal and nervous system activity is much the same for women as it is for men. However, other factors can inter-vene to make fight or flight less likely in women. Aggression in men, the researchers argue, is more likely to be regulated hormo-nally. In women, if aggression does occur it is more likely to be defined by circumstances and confined to specific situations that require defence. Similarly, immediate flight during times of danger would put offspring at risk.

Taylor and colleagues suggest that these gender differences are related in part to hormonal differences. Oxytocin, for example, promotes caregiving and underpins attachment. Under stress, some mothers appear to increase care and nurturing behaviours, suggesting an increase in oxytocin levels, and there is evidence that females prefer to seek out the company of others, especially other females. Making use of social support networks appears much less of a priority for males. What is equally evident is that men *do* use social networks for a whole variety of reasons.

Until fairly recently the assumed wisdom has always been that men tend to retreat into themselves during periods of stress and that very often this is accompanied by higher risk behaviours such as gambling, smoking, drinking, unsafe sex and drug use. Given that the tend-and-befriend model was only articulated in the late 1990s, it seems logical to refocus the spotlight on men.

A team of neuroscientists and psychologists at the University of Freiburg has overturned some long-held assumptions about male isolation and its association with stress. The team de-veloped a public-speaking task aimed to induce stress. Specially designed social-interaction games were then introduced, the aim of which was to measure positive social behaviours, such as trust and sharing, as well as negative behaviours. The male volunteers who undertook the public-speaking test behaved more positively than those who did not, while negative social behaviour was unaffected by stress. The team went on to report that positive social contact with a trusted individual before a stressful situ-ation reduces the stress response as much as during or immedi-ately after it.

This suggests that male emotional and behavioural reserves may run deeper than previously assumed. Greater male flexibility is good news and could suggest useful points for intervention. Stress, it now appears, can tease out men's gentler sides. The higher men's heart rates and cortisol levels are, the more trusting and friendly they become. Tend-and-befriend, it appears, is not exclusive to women.

Hypervigilance

From what I've said so far it seems that anxiety is not a single event. It is a process that involves various components embracing both the activation and experience of anxiety. People vary in their proneness to anxiety but a person who is vulnerable is also hypervigilant to surroundings, especially if the situation is new, relatively unfamiliar or potentially intimidating. Try the following questions:

- Do you experience difficulty getting to sleep at night?
- Do you find yourself waking up during the night?
- Could you easily fall asleep in a public place, somewhere like an airport or on a busy train?
- Do you find strangers easy company?
- Do you prefer not to have people stand or sit behind you?

If you answered 'yes' to most or all of these questions it would suggest you are hypervigilant, which makes perfect sense in the context of someone who is vulnerable to worry and anxiety. Here's an example.

Billy is a tall, athletic and physically fit 15-year-old who is being bullied at school. To avoid the bully he hangs back from the school gate until the last possible moment. When he moves from class to class he checks the corridors, moves rapidly and makes a point of never loitering. If he sees the bully he goes rigid. He feels his throat tighten and panic starts to set in. Even though the place he needs to be is just a few feet away he will either hide until the coast is clear or take the much longer route to avoid any contact.

The process of hypervigilance typically involves a rapid scan of a situation, which then narrows to a highly focused level of attention if a potential threat is spotted. Whatever the threat is (a person, social situation or object), it rapidly takes on a sharper and more defined quality and signals a change in behaviour. The person may find a reason to escape or avoid the threat, or if this is not possible may remain in a state of high arousal and attentiveness in which coping behaviours, often involving seeking something or someone to hold on to, may result.

Hypervigilance is characterized by increased physical and psychological arousal. Physical sensations, as mentioned previously, will typically include sweating, increased heart rate and rapid shallow breathing. Emotional concerns may lead to a whole variety of behaviours designed to help make the person feel more secure – for example, carrying a weapon for fear of assault, avoiding situations in which others sit behind him or her or being sensitive to sounds during the night and lying awake as a result.

Not surprisingly, hypervigilance is considered a common feature of various anxiety disorders, including post-traumatic stress disorder. In some cases it can be extreme enough for the person to become almost entirely preoccupied with scanning the environment for threats. He or she may become agitated in crowded or noisy places and may adopt a number of obsessive behaviour patterns as ways of coping.

Anxiety and panic attacks

The so-called anxiety attack is really the culminating moment of excessive worry over an issue. The symptoms, while somewhat similar to a panic event (panic attack), do differ enough to distinguish the two.

> Molly hasn't slept well. Despite extensive revision she feels poorly prepared for the exam. Outside the examination hall the other students chatter and laugh nervously. With ten minutes to go, Molly begins to feel fidgety. Her jaw muscles begin to tense and her legs go rigid. She feels her hands begin to shake and the more she tries to control the sensations the worse they seem to get. She feels dizzy, sick and short of breath.

The kinds of symptom Molly feels are severe enough for her to be noticed. A few calming words of reassurance will probably be sufficient for her to settle, and within a few minutes she will be able to confront the situation she so dreaded. Once seated, and with the examination under way, the stressor passes and so does the anxiety. This may be the one and only time Molly goes through such an experience or it may be the precursor to others in situations or events she associates with stress.

Anxiety attacks and panic attacks can seem so similar that some experts appear to have stopped distinguishing between the two. In the case of a panic attack there is a lack of any specific build-up to the moment of panic, and the attack tends to be far more severe – someone suffering such an attack may have all the symptoms previously outlined and more besides. A panic attack may appear to come out of the blue and with such severity that the person feels he or she is going crazy and is about to die. There is a genuine fear of dying, and the symptoms are quite frequently misinterpreted as a heart attack, often leading to an emergency hospital admission.

People who experience panic attacks tend to misinterpret bodily signs and focus very much on the moment, whereas those who experience anxiety attacks have very specific worrying events in their lives that have built up and reached a critical point. The build-up is slow, the nature of the anxiety is known and the symptoms of the attack less intense.

The four most commonly reported symptoms of panic are rapid heart beat, sweating, dizziness and shortness of breath. People with shortness of breath often go to great and frequently unpopular lengths to ensure that a supply of fresh air is available. They may, for example, drive with the window down in all weathers or insist that windows always be open at their home or place of work. The perception of such people as 'fresh-air freaks' is a price many are prepared to accept to mask the real reason behind their need.

Self-help for panic

A variety of successful treatment methods are available for all anxiety-related conditions – I go into these in more detail later on. Self-help for panic can be effective so long as you feel motivated to change and there are no additional issues such as depression that you are coping with. It's common for panic and agoraphobia to co-exist, so I'm accounting for this.

There are no hard and fast rules to these self-help ideas and my suggestion is that so long as you follow some basic principles you should find relief. Some people have said they get so absorbed in a new or rediscovered hobby that their anxiety simply seems to dissipate. Here are my tips.

- Cut out stimulants like coffee or caffeine-based energy drinks.
- Cut out alcohol.
- Introduce a regular sleep pattern with a good number of hours of uninterrupted sleep each night.
- Establish small goals that can be achieved. If you're uncomfortable leaving the house, maybe set a target for getting to the gate. If what you've set yourself feels manageable but just a little unsettling, you've probably hit the right target.
- Practise several times a day.
- Undertake some form of relaxation daily. You could even combine relaxation with exercise, such as yoga or t'ai chi. YouTube is a great archive of information and I've put some suggestions in the References section at the end of the book.
- Find a breathing technique that suits you. Essentially you need to ensure that your posture isn't constricting your lungs. Try this now:
  - Straighten up, place the palm of your hand on your stomach and breathe in slowly and fully, as though filling a glass.
  - If you can feel your hand move as your lungs fill with air that's good – it means you aren't just using the top of your lungs. You may feel a little light-headed doing this but it's only because of the extra oxygen you're drawing in.
  - When you breathe out, do so slowly and as though you have more air to breathe out than you took in.

There are similarities here between what happens to breathing during panic and what you see athletes doing before an event. Air is being pulled into the body rapidly, which floods it with oxygen and hormones ready for action. But with panic there is no outlet, so reversing the effect can have dramatic results. If you sense your-self building to a panic attack, try breathing in slowly and fully, holding your breath to a slow count of four, then breathing out slowly – again as if you have more air to remove than you drew in.

Hyperventilation

Overbreathing (hyperventilation) is as much a cause as it is a feature of panic. Typically it occurs in the form of rapid and fairly shallow breathing, which can quickly lead to dizziness and/ or light-headedness, plus other symptoms such as tingling in the fingers, a sense of pressure in and around the chest and a red face. It's little wonder these symptoms are frequently viewed as a heart attack both by the victim and sometimes by onlookers.

Assuming a heart attack or other conditions have been ruled out, the person may be referred for psychological assessment. As part of the assessment process she or he may be asked to undertake a hyperventilation test. This will not be conducted if the person has a medical background of epilepsy, high or low blood pressure, cardiovascular disease or asthma. The test will also be omitted if the person is pregnant.

If conducted, the test will help the therapist determine whether hyperventilation is a key cause of panic. The therapist asks the patient to breathe in a rapid and shallow fashion for up to two min-utes. Some form of anxiety assessment may precede the hyperven-tilation test. This typically involves a rating scale of 0–10 or 0–100, where the upper figure represents absolute fear or terror. Following the test, patients re-rate their anxiety. Usually the second rating reveals a higher level of anxiety and patients report very similar sensations to their previous experience of panic.

Some people are prone to repeated hyperventilation – two groups appear most affected. The first are those with asthma – previous and current – and the second are those who, for whatever reason, have a fear of suffocation. The conventional wisdom of asking someone in panic to breathe into a paper bag is based on the reasoning that carbon dioxide is too low as a result of overbreathing. In reality this technique is rarely if ever taught now. One reason is that people in a state of panic are rarely capable of breathing into a bag, and second, there are medical concerns as to whether the technique is actually counterproductive, particularly if a panic attack is confused with an asthma attack. In practice it is far more common for people to be taught how to control and regulate their breathing.

Vision

One of the more common effects of anxiety is eye strain or other forms of visual disturbance. This is nearly always related to the surge in adrenaline that accompanies anxiety, and it's worth outlining what's happening.

Primary and secondary forms of anxiety have different effects. Primary anxiety is that part of our fight-or-flight system that energizes us to deal with some threat. Our body floods with adrenaline, sugars, fats and other hormones to allow us to take action.

Secondary anxiety, by contrast, has no particular focus. It manifests itself in terms of worry and concerns over whether certain tasks or activities are within the grasp of the individual. It's hard to control, interferes with performance and can feed physical symptoms such as shaking, difficulty with walking, nausea, giddiness and distorted vision.

In the case of chronic stress and anxiety, the level of adrenaline within the body remains elevated. This can cause pressure on the eyes, sometimes resulting in blurred vision. Tunnel vision is another feature of excessive adrenaline. This tends to occur at times of high arousal or during a panic event.

Previously I described the features of hypervigilance. This actually affects all the senses but as far as vision is concerned, our pupils dilate in response to adrenaline in order to take in more of our surroundings. We become highly sensitized to any slight movement. Over time this, and the strain from other senses, can cause muscular tensions and headaches.

Some people with long-term anxiety find that wearing tinted lenses or sunglasses reduces light sensitivity. This seems to help with their anxiety and also helps to prevent headaches. Some prescription lenses have permanent tints or are a type that reacts to light. While some level of relief may be achieved this way, not everyone with anxiety wears tinted lenses for the same reason. Dark lenses can also act as a kind of social barrier, and while wearing them isn't really a solution to the problem, for some people they clearly seem to have a place. Dark or tinted lenses are used as a response to high arousal, so the emphasis should still be on trying to find ways to reduce this state of arousal.

Irritable bowel syndrome

You know what it's like when you're anxious and how your stomach knots up and lurches around? Well, one of the most common physical complaints associated with anxiety is irritable bowel syndrome (IBS). The NHS Choices website summarizes the most common symptoms of IBS as:

- abdominal pain and cramping – often relieved by emptying your bowels;
- a change in your bowel habits – such as diarrhoea, constipation or sometimes both;
- bloating and swelling of your abdomen;
- excessive wind (flatulence);
- an urgent need to go to the toilet;
- a feeling that you need to open your bowels even if you have just been to the toilet;
- a feeling you have not fully emptied your bowels;
- passing mucus from your bottom.

Anxiety, however, may not be the *cause* of IBS. In fact it still isn't really clear what the relationship is between IBS and anxiety, except that they often co-exist. We know, for example, that relief from stress can help to ease the symptoms associated with the syndrome. We also know that certain changes to diet and lifestyle can have positive effects.

The cause of IBS may not be known but its association with anxiety and stress and the lack of any obvious organic cause make it an easy target to be considered psychosomatic.

IBS – sometimes still described as spastic colon – is one of the commonest conditions affecting the gut, in as many as one in five adults. It affects more women than men and its symptoms may be mild or severe.

People who suffer from anxiety or stress can often associate an upsurge in gastric upsets with difficult times. These may be work-related, loneliness or even disrupted sleep and dietary patterns. Remove the problem and there may also be a corresponding reduction in gastric symptoms.

Sometimes it is our body that tells us things aren't right. If we're attuned to the changes and can join the dots, it may be easier to take some corrective action. Whether or not IBS results from stress is in some ways beside the point. For all we know it is the symptoms of IBS that add to anxiety, and so begins a vicious circle. We know the brain and the body have a complex and subtle relationship, so it seems reasonable to consider both in any therapy.

Self-help for IBS

If you have IBS you will probably already know the importance of diet and will have modified your diet according to your own preferences. There are several web-based resources that point to IBS-friendly diets. Helen Foster, for example, writing for NetDoctor. co.uk, provides 'The Anti-Irritable Bowel Syndrome Eating Plan', a seven-day eating schedule. Otherwise exercise, probiotics and stress-reduction techniques can all help.

Although not really in the self-help category, medication in the form of antispasmodics or laxatives for IBS-related constipation can also help.

Acute stress disorder

Vehicle collisions, rape, natural disasters and armed conflicts are just a few examples of the many unexpected and unwelcome traumas that can affect people for years. We cope with traumatic experiences in very different ways, and while some people appear able to adapt and move on, others have greater difficulty. A particular group of symptoms, characterized by a state of inner distancing from the trauma, has become known as acute stress disorder (ASD). Of central concern to some experts is that those who show symptoms of ASD are more likely to develop chronic post-traumatic stress disorder.

The symptoms of ASD include a reduced sense of awareness of surroundings and a feeling of numbness or detachment from the traumatic situation. People with ASD believe the circumstances around them aren't real (de-realization) and frequently refer to their feelings as like being in a dream. Sometimes there is a sense of being outside the situation, like observers looking in, not actually involved. It is as though they are floating above or around the situation but their bodies are in a different place altogether (depersonalization).

When asked to recall particular features of the original trauma, the sense of dissociation sometimes extends into memory. This seems to be some kind of protective mechanism whereby very significant aspects of the trauma become locked down. Such a form of localized amnesia is, however, a reversible condition.

People with ASD symptoms show all the early signs of post-traumatic stress disorder, and for this reason some experts question whether it is a unique condition in its own right. For a diagnosis of ASD to be made the aforementioned symptoms must be present, but also a minimum of one symptom associated with PTSD, such as:

- flashbacks of trauma;
- an active avoidance of reminders;
- increased vigilance, sleep disturbance, irritability, poor concentration and an exaggerated startle response.

As with most psychiatric diagnoses, there is a requirement that clinical distress extends beyond personal discomfort and in some way actively disrupts normal social and/or work functions. Further examples include aggressive or suicidal behaviour, self-harm and sexual dysfunction. Symptoms must last for a minimum of two days and a maximum of four weeks, and must occur within four weeks of the trauma.

Obsessional thinking

Obsessional thinking is a real personal battle. People understand the lack of logic behind their thinking and that their thought processes are of their own design, but also feel that this process is out of their control. Obsessional thinking tends to defy rational thought processes, and anxiety increases as a result.

Obsessional thoughts are unpleasant, unwelcome and repetitive. Common themes include harm being inflicted on other people, often close to the person concerned, sex, contamination from bacteria and viruses and bad language. Obsessive thoughts may also include the fear of making mistakes or behaving in some inappropriate way. There are some well-known obsessions, largely because the obsession (the thought process) frequently translates into a compulsion (some action) – for example, concerns over security (locked doors, gas turned off, light switches) and the need for exactness and arranging things in order or sequence.

Thought–action fusion is the term usually applied to a particular feature of obsessive thinking. Here people hold a belief that the more they think about something the greater the chance it will actually happen. For example, the more often they think of themselves being involved in a car accident the more likely it is to happen. This form of thinking is not so far removed from what is termed magical thinking; that is, a belief that certain actions will have consequences – usually negative.

Superstitions are an everyday example. Many otherwise perfectly rational individuals will not walk under a ladder or will get upset if they spill milk or crack a mirror. Spells and other mystical activities are a step up from this and appear to have a profound effect on susceptible individuals. Repeatedly thinking that something will happen sets up an internal conflict between the thoughts themselves and attempts to suppress them. This is one of the root causes of anxiety.

Appearance

Appearances matter, but for 1 in 100 people they seem to matter too much. Excessive worry about some minor or imagined issue with appearance is called body dysmorphic disorder (BDD), which has become a common mental-health problem.

We begin to pay more attention to our appearance during adolescence, so it's not surprising to learn that problems often start during this sensitive time. A lot of time may be spent gazing into the mirror, comparing our appearance with that of friends and celebrities and feeling self-conscious about blemishes, physical development and facial characteristics. All this is perfectly normal and most people manage to grow into their skin and accept things for what they are.

For others the situation is more complex. They become distressed and anxious about some perceived physical defect, a reaction others find far out of proportion. The focus of attention often relates to one or more features of the face but other parts of the body may also be involved. A great deal of time may be spent checking the mirror and using make-up in attempts to hide or diminish the perceived problem. In more extreme cases people may avoid social contact, be unable to establish relationships or maintain employment. They believe people are staring, talking or laughing about their situation, but this simply isn't the case.

BDD is more common in people who suffer with social phobia, generalized anxiety disorder or depression. It also occurs alongside eating disorders and obsessive–compulsive disorder. It is a highly distressing condition associated with very high levels of suicidal thoughts and suicide attempts. One investigation published in the *Journal of Clinical Psychiatry* found that 78 per cent of people with BDD experienced lifetime suicidal ideation (thoughts about suicide) and 27.5 per cent had attempted suicide. In fact completed suicide rates may be more than double those in clinical depression and 45 times higher than in the general US population, according to Phillips and Menard (2006).

The cause or causes of BDD are not fully understood. Explanations range from genetic predisposition, to neurotransmitter imbalances in the brain, to physical or emotional neglect. Some similarities exist between OCD and BDD, although current thinking suggests the conditions are different. People with BDD often repeatedly check their appearance in the mirror, can't relax unless they have removed and reapplied make-up or positioned hair so that it helps to cover a perceived problem.

The top five concerns of those with BDD are skin, hair, nose, weight and stomach. Cosmetic surgery may appear a likely solution to some of the problems but research conducted in 2010 by

Katherine Phillips found that only 2 per cent of procedures reduced BDD severity. In a survey of 265 cosmetic surgeons, 178 (65 per cent) reported treating patients with BDD, yet only 1 per cent of the cases resulted in BDD symptom improvement.

Sleep problems

We've probably all experienced times when our sleep is disrupted. If this happens occasionally then no real harm is done and we quickly make up the deficit. Worry, however, can intrude on sleep night after night, which disrupts our sleep pattern and can ultimately have health implications.

Two types of worrying affect sleep. The first is about things we've been unable to shake off or resolve during the day. The second involves worrying about sleep itself, or more accurately, getting enough sleep. Like many of you reading this, I've experienced both and can truly say that neither has ever solved a problem or made me feel better. I suppose there may have been times in the still of the night when I've achieved a moment of clarity, but these must be so rare that I can't actually recall them!

Overall I'm fortunate in having experienced relatively few sleepless nights. When I was much younger my problem was likely to be getting to sleep. Then I'd reach a point where I'd start to think, 'I really must get to sleep', and we all know where that leads. Some people have problems with staying asleep. There can be any number of reasons for sleep problems but if worry is the main culprit, what can be done?

So far as worry is concerned I can offer a couple of ideas. Exchanging one form of worry for another isn't going to help, so instead of worrying about not sleeping try focusing your attention on relaxing. If you know how to undertake relaxation breathing exercises, or progressive relaxation, so much the better – use those techniques.

Breaking into the no-sleep cycle is the technique I probably used the most. It may seem counterintuitive to leave your warm bed behind but this can be very effective. Make yourself a warm drink – not a stimulant like coffee – and relax in a chair surrounded by low lighting levels. Don't switch on the television and definitely don't switch on your computer. Don't do anything – and that includes reading, unless the book you have is spectacularly dull. After 30 minutes, go back to bed.

Here are a few more quick tips.

- Keep the bedroom cool and well ventilated.
- Alcohol can send you to sleep easily enough but you may find yourself awake a short time later, so this is best avoided.
- If you're a clock-watcher, it may be worth moving your clock to where you can't see it.
- Don't go to bed on an empty stomach or a very full one.
- Daytime naps shouldn't really be necessary if you're getting enough sleep at night. Try to cut them out or reduce the duration.

4

Work and lifestyle

Work worries

When it comes to worrying, the world of work is often a central focus, partly because it can be such an unforgiving place, although sometimes it just seems that way. In our day-to-day dealings we generally accept a little nervousness in others, but employees who exhibit anxiety during business exchanges, presentations or social gatherings send out the wrong message. It's bad for business.

In most work environments people follow codes of accepted behaviour. Sometimes these codes take a little while to master. Some are overt and can be embedded as a part of company policy – no shouting or swearing, for example. Others are more subtle and unwritten and involve anything from never using Jack's mug to the boss's raising of an eyebrow to signal displeasure.

The thing about a successful interpersonal environment is that it represents a form of trade: you offer me something and I'll offer something in return; I offer you a coffee and you accept or graciously decline. These interactions lubricate our social wheels and encourage us to believe that future interactions will go well. However, if one or both people are anxious it can lead to clumsy or inappropriate statements or behaviours. This in turn may cause a collapse in the interaction that can lead to embarrassments, further anxiety or even hostility.

Coping with our own anxiety is one thing but coping with other people's requires additional skills. We can't necessarily see anxiety in other people but it is often easy to infer its presence. So what are the consequences? Anxiety often comes across as irritation, but if we meet this with our own irritation the situation is more likely to escalate. Then again, if we make attempts to understand others' irritation it can come across as patronizing. Therefore to sustain a relationship with anxious people the general rule is to empathize and offer reassurance while ensuring you achieve what you need.

This last statement isn't intended to sound heartless but we do need to distinguish our role in work. Are we employed as a therapist? Well, probably not, unless it's in our job description. Is part of our role to get on with colleagues yet achieve our goals? The answer to that one will probably be 'yes'.

Personal anxieties are often fuelled by self-destructive inner conversations about lack of worth, skills and inadequacies. We can chip away at personal anxieties by focusing our energies on behaving in a more relaxed and confident manner. This alone helps some people. For others it's more important that they become involved with the inner conversation because this is the cause of their confidence becoming eroded.

What do I mean by an inner conversation? Well, it's all those negative beliefs you hold about yourself – such as that you aren't experienced, capable or clever enough to express an opinion; that if you say or do something, everyone will think you're stupid; that you may offend or upset others or cause them to laugh at you, and so on.

It was Mark Twain who observed that his life had been full of troubles, but most of them had never happened. We all have strengths and limitations but our self-belief governs which of these dominate our thinking and therefore our anxieties.

Performance anxiety

So many work roles now require different forms of presentational skill. The everyday term associated with performance-related anxiety is stage fright. Although it reveals itself in different ways, people's stage fright fears are really quite consistent. The greatest fear for people is showing signs of anxiety, such as trembling or having a shaky voice. Fear of the mind going blank, freezing and being unable to continue, saying or doing something embarrassing or saying something stupid, are also high on the agenda.

In principle there isn't such a difference between talking to one person and talking to several. Granted, more of a two-way interaction is expected with just two people, but beyond this the difference between speaking to two or, say, two hundred is a matter of scale and a difference in direction. Whether we talk to one person or to many we engage in a process in which both the speaker and those who listen have goals. In a successful delivery, goals are met; but if anxiety inhibits the process neither the speaker nor the audience is satisfied. Anxiety is infectious and it results in frustration.

The root of stage fright is a kind of internal dialogue that becomes handicapping. It goes along the same lines I've previously mentioned, namely not feeling experienced or clever enough to do this.

Aside from the actual skill of presentation, those with stage fright fear the negative evaluation of others and being the centre of attention. When they do begin their presentation they may further handicap themselves by apologizing in advance. It sets up a negative experience for their audience, who are left feeling tense on behalf of the speaker and/or concerned they are about to get a poor deal.

Pretty much all the advice you will come across about stage fright says the same thing about the need for preparation. If you haven't got the basics together, you stand a far higher chance of things going wrong.

A useful blog I read on the website Psychologytoday.com was entitled 'Fighting Stage Fright'. The article cites Joseph O'Connor, the Irish writer who, it seems, suggests five minutes of preparation for every minute of presentation. Also, practise speaking out loud so that you become accustomed to the sound of your own voice. Time yourself and maybe get someone to listen to you and offer feedback.

The same article suggests exaggerating your own symptoms. So if you suffer from shaking, try to make your hands shake more. The author claims you will find that your hands then stop shaking. The principle here is that if you are able to increase symptoms you are able to control them.

Arriving early at the venue is frequently regarded as a good thing. It allows you to become familiar with the space and the equipment. If you are among the first to arrive you effectively 'own' the space others will then enter. Arrive last and it's a bit like having to enter any crowded space in that, for many people, it's just a little more difficult.

If you've done your preparation you should find things go pretty smoothly. Nobody expects or even listens out for a slick presentation. How many times have you heard newsreaders having to retrace something they've said? All those years of practice and they're still prone to stumbling and making errors. We all do it, so if you find yourself in the situation, take the time to get back on course and don't get flustered.

Perfectionism

Most people won't admit to being an out-and-out perfectionist. For one thing it makes them sound just a little weird and for another it makes them fallible to imperfections. Therefore it's more acceptable and much more common to hear something along the lines of: 'I'm a bit of a perfectionist, but only where work is concerned.'

And here's the problem. It's a rare thing to find someone who is a 'work perfectionist' but can switch off to become someone else at the end of the day. It's far more likely that the issues of the working day intrude into leisure time. Perfectionists are often at work even when they're supposedly having days off or taking a vacation – they may not have papers or a computer in front of them but their minds are churning over past decisions and actions to a point where quality of life is affected.

There are different aspects to perfectionism that seem to work for or against us. It clearly works to our advantage to know that surgeons or aircraft pilots set high standards for their work. But it isn't helpful for those same people to maintain such precise standards in their family life, where it can lead to dysfunctional relationships.

Not surprisingly, perfectionists are known to worry and suffer from stress, and there is some evidence that high perfectionists die younger, although only in certain circumstances. For example, the psychologist Prem Fry found that perfectionists with type 2 diabetes have a much lower risk of death from diabetes because of the attention to detail they apply to management of their disease.

Many people set high standards for themselves yet have perfectly well-balanced lives. The real problem is when people start to worry about mistakes. It is the ruminating concerns that something could have been done better, may have been overlooked or hasn't been properly finished that gnaw away at some people. This concern with mistakes seems to be a key area that differentiates excellence from perfectionism.

Of central concern to perfectionists is the fear that if they give up their way of thinking and behaving, things will start to fall apart. Many have the intellectual insight to know that perfectionism can actually harm performance more than it helps, but perfectionism is so integral to their sense of self-worth it's hard to let go.

Burnout and rust-out

Now we turn to the other side of the coin. Once, perhaps, you were a high achiever. You were full of enthusiasm and energy about your work. You'd willingly put in the hours and more besides. You'd worry about standards, defend your work, extol its virtues and you felt part of something bigger than yourself.

Then somewhere along the line all this began to change. At first you maybe put it down to feeling a bit tired and a little out of sorts, but new feelings and thoughts slowly took up residence. Increasingly you began to question the worth of what you were doing and that your hard work seemed to be taken for granted. Now it's easy to see the cracks in the system and your thoughts and perhaps your conversations have become increasingly cynical. You notice how you've become detached, tired and irritated by the tasks you have to accomplish. In short, you have all the symptoms of burnout.

The psychologist Herbert J. Freudenberger is generally credited with coining the term burnout and defining it as 'the extinction of motivation or incentive, especially where one's devotion to a cause or relationship fails to produce the desired results'. The sense of trying harder while seeming to achieve less is a central feature of burnout.

It was Freudenberger who also commented on the sense of 'omnipotence' that frequently accompanies those in the situation of burnout. Even if offered, they are likely to refuse help from other people in the belief that only they have the capabilities for the job –

and this despite the fact that their work may have become sloppy and fallen behind schedule.

The physical and emotional exhaustion associated with burnout can manifest itself in terms of suspicion of other people's motives, depression and an increase in psychosomatic symptoms, such as headache, backache, difficulty sleeping and stomach complaints. People with burnout become more irritable, inflexible, critical and reluctant to view themselves as having a problem, but the situation simply worsens if ignored.

More enlightened companies recognize that burnout is commonly associated with people in positions of authority who have simply worked too hard for too long. Some such companies have even established systems for recognizing and working with individuals or groups who either suffer from or are at risk of burnout. For the individual, however, the first step in reversing the effects of burnout is to recognize the signs. Once this is done, a few very simple techniques can help to reverse the process.

By contrast, you may be involved in a job that is unrewarding, repetitive and just plain boring. You feel restless, unhappy, stuck in a rut. Perhaps you find yourself grumbling to co-workers, friends and family.

Rust-out is the term occupational psychologists give to symptoms arising from jobs that leave people feeling apathetic, uninterested and dull. Effectively it's the opposite of burnout, yet some of the effects appear remarkably similar. Productivity slows, mistakes increase and quality suffers, at least in jobs where such things can be seen or measured. Other jobs are mind-numbing, simple and repetitive, and it may be harder to spot rust-out other than perhaps from increased sickness and absence.

The common factor with burnout and rust-out is stress. With burnout there is simply too much stress but with rust-out there isn't enough positive stress to keep the person interested. Regular and sustained levels of boredom are actually highly stressful.

These days the hierarchies of many big organizations have been reduced (I believe the current term is 'flattened'). Also, many previously complex jobs have become automated and streamlined. This has a couple of effects. The first is that opportunities for promotion become more limited, resulting in often well-qualified and highly motivated young people working in jobs in which there is little or no scope for advancement and undertaking tasks that are unfulfilling and sometimes demeaning relative to their capabilities. Second, older people in more middle-management posts who find themselves unable to advance simply see themselves going through the motions and counting off the days until they can retire.

The problem can be tackled from two directions. First, employees who feel underwhelmed by work can consider varying their own activities or approaching their employer to request new responsibilities. If, as is possibly the case, these simply don't exist, the only real course of action left is to seek different employment.

A second possible direction for change is for managers to become more aware of the likelihood of rust-out in their organization. They might, for example, vary or rotate tasks in order to maintain interest. They might take the time to match employees to the correct level of job and to spot talent that might be languishing in some easily overlooked places. Involving employees in new projects, testing ideas and decision-making, helps them feel valued and useful.

City living

The number of people living in cities continues to grow. Some estimates are that around 70 per cent of people are likely to live in cities by the year 2050. City living provides a rich, stimulating, social and cultural environment as well as easy access to medical care and a range of other facilities. The downside is that the risk of suffering from anxiety disorders is 21 per cent higher than for those who live in more rural settings, and 39 per cent higher for mood disorders.

Findings from an international research study published in the journal *Nature* demonstrate that certain regions of the brain involved with emotion regulation and stress are sensitive to the experience of city living. Using a series of MRI scanning experiments, researchers compared the effects of an induced stress task in volunteers from both rural and urban areas. Those living in urban areas showed much higher stress responses. Dr Jens Pruessner of the Douglas Mental Health University Institute in Quebec, who helped run the study, also said the incidence of schizophrenia is almost doubled for individuals born and brought up in cities. It isn't yet clear why these areas of the brain are more active in city dwellers but possible candidates for consideration are toxins, crowding and noise.

One reason why some people appear to thrive in cities while others yearn to leave may be the degree of perceived control individuals have over their daily lives. Plus, of course, cities tend to have higher rates of crime and certain areas that are more no-go than others.

Technology

The dream of technology setting us free has turned into something of a nightmare – or maybe I'm just betraying my age. Technology promised to speed our work, help us make fewer mistakes, enhance our lives and increase our free time.

In my lifetime we've moved from a situation in which work was work and free time began when work finished. It made things very simple and the lines were clear for all to see. Today we're having expert seminars on the importance of work–life balance. Is it just a little alarming that we're having to be taught that free time is important?

We're besotted with technology. Access to mobile devices and the internet is viewed by many as a basic need. There are now people on the planet who've never physically written a letter or a memo, except by email. And the days when memos slowly stacked up on the desk and you took a fortnight to answer them have gone. Happy days!

Work now travels around with us. The day off is becoming an increasingly odd concept and, worst of all, away from the devices, the texts and emails, some people get really anxious. It's a curious thing. Technology often provides the illusion of freedom that allows us to do things when we want. In reality our quality of life is gradually eroding because of the technology we love.

Technology, quality of life and personal identity

How do we measure quality of life? Actually there are many ways, but I'm turning to the state of Bhutan for this measure, simply because I love it. How many other countries can you think of that use a measure of 'gross national happiness' in order to measure the well-being of the nation? Brilliant! Effectively it averages out seven 'well-being metrics' that include physical, mental, work, social, economic, political and environmental aspects of well-being. Bhutan in fact ranked eighth out of 178 countries in subjective well-being, and is the only country in the top 20 'happiest' countries that has a very low GDP.

Some psychologists and social observers say we're probably much more resentful and unhappy than ever before, despite the affluence many of us enjoy. The build-up of daily resentments, sarcasm, cynicism and stress are a toxic mix. The upshot of this is that we're increasingly less open and approachable and more anxious and hostile. A possible consequence is that it becomes easier to gain sometimes hundreds of 'friends' on social networking sites. We can wear our hearts on our sleeve as easily as we can toss people to one side in this anonymous world.

Does technology fuel our interests and needs or does it simply meet them? Online messaging, tweets and texts create the illusion of community, but face-to-face community takes a bit of effort and is ultimately a more enriching and rewarding experience. Professor Jim Taylor wonders whether technology is beginning to steal our self-identities. He makes the case that most social forces in previous generations were largely positive – parents, peers, schools, communities and even the media.

Professor Taylor argues that, 'today, popular culture manufactures "portraits" of who it wants us to be. The problem is that the self-identity that is served by popular culture serves its own best interests rather than what is best for us.' It follows that people heavily involved in social media start to see their identity in terms of what they would like it to be and what they feel others want to see. The development of our own personality takes second place as we conform to the requirements of a digital world.

I know technology for some people is life enhancing and sometimes even life critical. For others, does their use of technology help to diffuse responsibility, lower expectations, reduce effort and ultimately make them unhappy and more bitter? It's a big debate and no doubt people have strong views about the role and nature of technology in our lives.

Mobile devices

My nephew has a Homer Simpson ringtone. It's configured so that when he receives a call from work it goes 'Doh!' but when it's from a friend or family it goes 'Woo-hoo!'. It makes us laugh and it's useful because it acts as a filter. Unless he's expecting an especially important call, the ones from work are ignored during his free time.

Our phones and other mobile devices have increasingly become a part of our very fabric – so much in fact that in 2008 the term nomophobia was conjured up to reflect the fear and anxiety of being without them. Nomophobics are those people who can't be without their mobile phone, who can't switch it off at night, who check for texts or messages several times an hour and who get physical symptoms like increased heart rate and sweating if their phone goes missing.

I may be accused of being picky when I suggest the anxiety connected with loss of a mobile phone doesn't really fall into the phobia category. To me, the need for mobile-phone use and checking is more a sign of dependency that can lead to compulsive checking acts. In saying that I'm signed up to the idea that phone use does, in some form, act as a barometer of anxiety, but the reasons vary from person to person, and age also makes a difference. Loss of a phone may well cause great anxiety but again I think there are a host of reasons why. Maybe the statistics for so-called nomophobia have increased because our mobile devices are now more expensive, more complex, contain more personal information, photographs, videos and documents than they ever did, or could, in 2008.

Even so, I think they are great. They can provide us with maps, tell us where the nearest coffee place is, take pictures, contain addresses and pretty much anything we used to consider as the exclusive function of the home computer. It's rare to embrace a technology without finding some darker side in terms of the costs we must pay – for example, the use of a phone as a surveillance device. But are mobile devices helpful for anxiety or do they make things worse?

The days when older children might step out of the door and be told what time they needed to be back have pretty much passed. Today kids and teens may still go off for the day but their mobile phone is likely to be with them. Not uncommonly their very first one will be a gift from parents who view it as a means of keeping in touch and ensuring everything is all right. To what extent do children pick up the message that their phone is a gift because their parents are concerned about their welfare?

Those with a mobile phone quickly realize it can be used for and in a variety of reasons or situations, one of which is when anxiety strikes. Maybe they call when walking alone, in a taxi or in a crowd of people they don't know or among whom they feel uncomfortable. Sometimes rather than learning to cope with social situations or even a touch of boredom, the phone is available as a handy form of displacement or distraction.

The fact that mobile devices are also used to connect to social media brings a whole new set of issues into the worrying frame. Every day, for example, we learn of vulnerable young people becoming the victims of so-called troll abuse and bullying.

5

Medical and related anxieties

Cyberchondriasis

Since medical knowledge became freely available to anyone with an internet connection, the urge to seek out answers to symptoms has increased. The term cyberchondria, the internet 'equivalent' to hypochondria, reflects the fact that roughly two per cent of all web searches are health-related, and that around one third of surfers escalate their search to investigate serious illnesses.

Hypochondriasis refers to imagined diseases or conditions that cause significant anxiety and distress. The condition tends to develop in people around their mid twenties to thirties and appears equally distributed between men and women. If left unchecked the condition can develop into an all-consuming obsession in which normal bodily sensations are taken to be symptoms of terrible diseases.

So are you a cyberchondriac? According to Arthur J. Barsky, the author of *Worried Sick: Our Troubled Quest for Wellness*, illness is central to the identity of the hypochondriac. If you find yourself latching on to serious illnesses that frequently have ambiguous symptoms such as lethargy, flu-like symptoms, headaches and so on, you could be something of a cyberchondriac.

During a Microsoft study into how people use the web, one of the issues identified is that search engines don't discriminate between minor and major illnesses. People who type in the word 'headache' are as likely to uncover material about rare brain tumours as they are about other more common causes.

The problem for cyberchondriacs or people heading in that direction is that they frequently focus on reputable medical websites. This leads to a furthering of anxieties as they find symptoms that appear to match their own. Health anxieties are thought to cost billions each year in unnecessary tests and sometimes treatments.

Dental and medical anxieties

Medical procedures vary greatly in extent of intrusiveness and complexity. Despite this, even the simplest procedures may generate high levels of anxiety in some people. Unfamiliar surroundings and smells, strange people speaking in jargon and lack of understanding about what is happening and why are just some of the reasons people feel under stress.

Some medical procedures require little more than taking a tablet. Some are painful, some intimate, some difficult and lengthy. Many will leave patients with little or no control over what is happening to them. As patients the way we cope with such situations depends on a variety of factors. Previous experience and knowledge can make a big difference, although in some situations a little knowledge may be almost as bad as too much. Generally though, our age, gender and the social and cultural context with which we are familiar have a big influence over how well we are prepared to take action in order to reduce anxiety in medical situations.

Some early studies into the needs and expectations of patients were simple but interesting. Typically both patients and health professionals would be asked to rank a list of things felt to be most or least important to patients during a stay in hospital. It was quickly discovered that the priority lists for patients were in stark contrast to those assumed by health professionals. A lot has been learned since then, most notably that patients' perspectives should have priority when it comes to helping them cope with anxiety in the order and at the speed they require.

Helping people cope with the anxiety of medical procedures is a two-way street. Health professionals need to know the type of information that is necessary and that will be of benefit, but they need to tailor this to the needs and capabilities of individuals.

For the sake of argument let's assume the patient is about to undergo some surgical procedure, although it could just as well be a course of radiotherapy or, say, ECT for depression. Four broadly overlapping types of information will be of benefit. The first of these is simple factual information about the procedure(s) and what will happen. The second is how this will make the person feel – for example, perhaps it is worth knowing that it is perfectly normal to feel sick following anaesthetic. The third relates to any particular emotions that may be evoked. The fourth relates to a time frame for recovery – although not strictly related to the procedure, it is important for patients to know how long they may be out of action as a result of their condition.

With all these issues, effective communication is the key to helping reduce anxiety. Not all patients like to ask questions and not all know what questions to ask. It shouldn't be assumed that silence equates to satisfaction. Neither should it be assumed that information imparted has been remembered or understood. Even the most relaxed and intelligent people can find themselves overwhelmed with information and terminology. As much as information can help reduce anxiety it must be remembered that anxiety also serves to block information. For this reason time, careful use of language and checking that information is understood are essential skills for caregivers in helping patients cope with anxiety.

Dental phobia

Some common questions concerning dental anxiety revolve around whether someone suffers with anxiety or phobia. In fact the gap between anxiety and phobia is somewhat blurred. Typically a phobia is considered an irrational fear that leads to avoidance or escape, so by that definition all who worry about their appointment but manage to haul themselves to the dentist aren't really phobic, although they may feel highly anxious.

The reasonableness or otherwise of anxiety varies from person to person. If you're in my 50-plus age bracket you'll probably remember when dentistry was not without its painful moments. In fact your anxiety about visits to the dentist probably still revolves around the prospect of pain. It's only a couple of years ago that I had a wisdom tooth removed, and despite sitting calmly in the waiting room I can assure you my pulse rate was anything but calm. In many respects dental surgery is no different from any other form of surgery. People naturally feel anxious in the run-up to treatment and relieved when it's over. However, perhaps you have a genuine terror of dental treatments or examinations.

Dental phobia isn't just about the fear of pain. It often involves deep-seated control issues in which we have no say or control over the procedure, the time it takes or when something might cause discomfort. We may fear the dental examination room itself, the lights, the noise of pumps and drills, the way dentists are dressed and masked. We may fear the intrusion of things into the mouth, choking, being sick or just the proximity of the dentist and his or her assistant to our face during a procedure.

Of course if fear of the dentist keeps people away there's a problem brewing. The chances of dental decay and gum disease increase, and with this general health can be affected. Rotten teeth are not nice to see or to have. They can increase anxiety, affect self-esteem, and the longer the situation goes on the more embarrassing and difficult it becomes.

Increasingly, dental practices put time and resources aside to treat dental phobia. They work at the pace of their patient and will address any fears the person may have. Dental phobia is highly responsive to treatment and many dental surgeons are trained and highly skilled in helping patients overcome their fears.

6

Thinking about therapy

So far we've established that some level of anxiety is perfectly normal. It's also something of a necessary evil that serves to prevent us taking too many risks and making too many bad decisions. Yet anxiety can also intrude into our lives in a way and to an extent that results in distress or illness. The chances are that you are reading this book for that very reason.

The fact that you have reached a point where treatment is being seriously considered tells me what a courageous person you are. You are in the process of making a conscious decision to improve your quality of life and you are investing your time, energy and emotions in the task. I can reassure you that your investment will not be wasted.

Worry and anxiety are usually very responsive to treatment so there's every reason for optimism – if you invest fully. For therapy to succeed it will almost certainly require your motivation and commitment. I know this won't be easy for you. Everything about your anxiety is telling you to avoid or escape from situations that make you feel uncomfortable and distressed. But you're already so unhappy that it's difficult to see how things could be worse.

I've tended to describe anxiety as if it is a single problem but actually there are different types and your treatment may vary according to your own circumstances. The main anxiety disorders are:

- specific phobia, in which one object or situation – such as heights, flying, dogs – is the focus of fear and tends to be avoided;
- panic disorder, in which intense fear is accompanied by physical symptoms and a fear of death or loss of control;
- generalized anxiety disorder, in which the person feels anxious about a variety of issues for lengthy periods of time;

- social phobia, in which the feared situation is with others and the person feels he or she is being judged;
- health anxiety, in which the fear is illness- or disease-focused;
- obsessive–compulsive disorder, in which intrusive thoughts require some form of ritual or repeated behaviour to be carried out;
- post-traumatic stress disorder, in which the direct or indirect experience of trauma makes the person anxious and vigilant.

The Improving Access to Psychological Therapies (IAPT) website provides a flowchart to help identify the specific anxiety disorder you may be experiencing – see <www.iapt.nhs.uk/silo/files/iapt-data-handbook-appendicies-v2.pdf>, Appendix C.

Now we move to the issue of treatment itself. The obvious first step for most of us is to visit the doctor, but I know this isn't a choice everyone wants to make. You may have all sorts of reasons not to. Perhaps you have a view about medications. Perhaps you've already tried this route and not found it to your liking. There may be a host of other reasons. My own view is that you probably should visit your family doctor, especially if you've never had your anxiety symptoms assessed. Anxiety can be a symptom of a number of physical conditions; if these are identified and treated, the symptoms of your anxiety will naturally be alleviated.

If you've already been down the medical route you may want to explore other options. My feeling is that therapy is multi-faceted. Many people find the greatest benefit, especially in the early stages, from mixing approaches. So you may find that medication in combination with psychological therapy is more beneficial than either in isolation.

There are many different types of therapy but you shouldn't be put off or feel nervous about whether or not you're choosing the right one. In this regard I have pinned my colours to the mast, so to speak, by declaring what I believe to be some of the most effective treatment options. I'll expand on these in more detail a little later.

You must also be wondering about the likely effects and outcome of therapy. Over the years I've been asked many questions about different types of therapy and what to expect.

- How long?
- How much?
- Which is best?
- Will I be cured?
- Does it hurt?
- Do I have to disclose personal information?
- Do I have to tell my boss?
- Is it really just mind control?

These are just a few, but a common thread is where all this leads. You may feel the ideal outcome of therapy choice is for you to be cured of anxiety. Unfortunately that won't happen because none of us can live a life without anxiety. For one thing, as I've said, it protects us. But you should reasonably expect to be able to overcome worry and anxiety to an acceptable degree and in a way that does not dominate your life. To my mind that's a good result.

Successful therapy depends on a number of things, but a key ingredient is you. You will get out what you put in. If you invest yourself fully it is perfectly reasonable for you to expect a relief from symptoms and a sense of greater empowerment and control over your life. Of course life will always throw up problems, but your ability to cope, rather than worry and fret, will improve and keep on improving over time.

Getting the best from therapy

Your therapist, should you choose to work with one, may technically be highly qualified, but if you can't connect and feel comfortable with her or him, it's not a good sign. If you go as a private client there's more choice, but if you've been referred for therapy by your doctor, your choices are likely to be limited because NHS resources are stretched. Even so, your own preferences might very well be taken into account because therapists know only too well the importance of the therapeutic relationship.

So what might you want to consider? Well, would you be happy with a therapist who is very much younger than you, or would you prefer someone the same age or older? Might you prefer a female therapist over a male? Would it be useful to have a therapist with a similar background – say from the armed forces?

Perhaps you'd prefer not to go down the face-to-face route. Telephone and online mental-health interventions, emails or video-conferencing are possible alternatives (more on this in the next chapter). The counselling provider Relate, for example, offers both telephone and online counselling – see <www.relate.org.uk>. At the time of writing the charge for a one hour standard telephone session with a Relate-trained counsellor is £40.

7

Guided and supportive therapies

Wherever there's a health problem you're almost bound to find a solution, or something claiming to be one. Over the next two chapters I'll provide insights into just a few of the therapies and remedies considered to alleviate the symptoms of anxiety. Some of these are well researched, with a strong evidence-base as to their effectiveness, others less so. In this chapter I'll provide you with some insights into the main approaches in which treatment for worry and anxiety is guided, shaped or directed by a therapist.

Western cultures have developed a strong tendency to externalize treatments. We rub on ointments, take tablets, inhale sprays and swallow liquids, for example. These methods are often quick, sometimes effective and don't require much from us in terms of cost or effort. What's more, we tend to have faith in such things, probably much more than we have in ourselves as agents of change. But none of these approaches is especially effective when it comes to treating anxiety, particularly in the long term, because this requires a form of treatment that comes from inside ourselves.

Don't misunderstand me – I do think medication has a place in relieving the symptoms of anxiety, but I also know it can never stop you from worrying and it certainly won't get to the bottom of why you're anxious. There may be circumstances where anxiety medication alone is sufficient to get you over a bad patch, but where anxiety is a long-term feature its effectiveness is likely to be limited to the length of time you take it.

It's not my intention to list the various anti-anxiety medications with their effects and side effects. You can very easily find this information via any online search engine. What I will say is that medication might be right for you if your anxiety is so severe that you simply can't function properly. If used in combination with psychotherapy, the effects may be even more beneficial.

But I'm guessing you want to know the alternatives to medication and the longer-term solutions. Well, the good news is there are several perfectly viable alternatives to medication that come without the risks and the side effects. What's more, it's only the psychological therapies that will help provide you with lifelong solutions to your anxiety problems.

When it comes to the so-called talking therapies, there are many options. The Department of Health – the part of UK government responsible for health care – provides a list of over 40 psychological therapies, which is a lot to get your head around. Fortunately, the National Institute for Health and Care Excellence (NICE) has the job of reviewing all the available evidence about treatments for physical and mental conditions; it then provides guidance about which treatments should be used. This is highly significant with regard to psychological therapies, and one in particular – cognitive behavioural therapy (CBT).

Cognitive behavioural therapy

Because of its importance I plan to spend some time describing CBT. First, CBT figures large in the NICE guidelines for the treatment of anxiety disorders and moderate to severe depression – which means that it works. In fact it's generally regarded as one of the most effective treatments available for worry, anxiety disorders and depression – see <www.iapt.nhs.uk/silo/files/iapt-data-handbook-appendicies-v2.pdf>, Appendix B.

There are a number of other reasons to commend CBT:

- It has a proven track record that is still developing.
- Success rates for all psychological conditions are good.
- It is inexpensive and often of relatively short duration – as few as 6 sessions lasting around an hour for mild cases, but usually 10–20 sessions.
- It is empowering and effective as a self-help strategy and provides skills – a toolkit – for use well after therapy has concluded.
- It is safe and natural and there are no side effects.
- It is increasingly being offered as an online option.

The most common approach is one-to-one with a therapist, but CBT can be offered as a part of group therapy, a self-help book or as an interactive (computerized) programme of CBT (CCBT), such as:

- Beating the Blues – see <www.beatingtheblues.co.uk>
- Fear Fighter – see <www.fearfighter.com>
- Living Life to the Full Interactive – see <www.llttfi.com>.

These are currently approved for use by the NHS and may be prescribed by your GP and supervised by her or him or an appropriate practitioner. These are effective and useful options to consider if the idea or the practicalities of meeting regularly with a therapist don't suit.

So how does CBT work? CBT is a treatment approach based around the relationship between thoughts – cognitions – and the behaviours stemming from these. By focusing on particular thoughts and beliefs known to affect your mood and behaviour negatively, your therapist, should you use one, collaborates with you to overcome your problem(s). The intention of the therapy is to reveal how your beliefs, thoughts and ways of coping co-exist in a kind of vicious circle. The aim thereafter is to establish alternative and more adaptive ways of coping.

CBT is based around four general principles:

1 Your anxiety is due to interpreting situations, people or events as more dangerous or threatening than they actually are.
2 Your thoughts, feelings, symptoms and behaviour are interlinked.
3 You will benefit from a clear understanding of the factors that keep you feeling anxious.
4 You need to make changes in order to reduce your anxiety.

Structure is a key ingredient. If you choose to go down the CBT route you'll find there are no couches to lie on and no encouraging you to talk about whatever comes to mind while the therapist takes notes. This doesn't mean it's cold and heartless. Structure is known to be one of the most helpful aspects of therapy, and because CBT is time-limited it provides an essential beginning, middle and end.

Emily is a bag of nerves. She used to run a small cake-baking business but the tension and stress that came with it got too much. She knows she should have delegated more, but the perfectionist in her meant she'd do things herself and end up baking, helping with deliveries and running the business.

Emily has a teenage daughter who gets frustrated with her mum. She's always getting text messages from her mum asking how she is, where she is and whether she's all right. It's embarrassing in front of her friends, but if she doesn't answer or turns off the phone, her mum goes ballistic with worry!

'Why do you text your daughter so much?' the therapist asks. Emily confesses that she worries constantly about her daughter's welfare when she's out. She thinks of all the terrible things that might happen to her, then she tries to predict how best to handle these situations, what she might say and do and where it might lead. It's exhausting, Emily says, and it's why she wants help.

Emily has generalized anxiety disorder, which I have discussed in Chapters 1 and 2. It's uncertainty that fuels her worry, and she becomes overwhelmed by thoughts of terrible things that might happen.

Emily's therapist will want to set some treatment goals, but for these to make sense, Emily will be asked to monitor and record her worrying over a week or so using a diary or possibly some recording sheets. The sorts of things Emily will record are:

- when and where she worries the most;
- things she worries about most often;
- recurring worry themes;
- whether worries are real or imagined.

Working with the therapist, Emily is then shown that her worry reveals three things. First, that uncertainty feeds worry and therefore anxiety. Second, worries fall into either a real or imagined category. If real, a problem-solving approach is needed, but if imagined, an approach that tackles worry is best. Third, it is Emily's beliefs about worry that help to maintain those worries.

Now the therapist will work with Emily to establish some treatment goals. These, the therapist says, should be SMART:

Specific
Measurable
Achievable
Realistic
Time limited

This means a goal such as 'I just want to stop worrying' is unattainable and impractical. In Emily's case one of her more realistic goals might be: 'To stop sending texts to my daughter when she's out and to find ways of coping with my worry when she's out'. Emily will then develop her remaining goals according to her unique circumstances and needs.

Having set her goals Emily now moves to the therapy stage. In collaboration with her therapist Emily will now be reviewing the homework tasks she was set between sessions. The chances are that she has been increasing her exposure to uncertainty and learning how to tolerate it by finding situations that actually stimulate uncertainty. In the first instance Emily might practise not checking for text messages every five minutes, or even turning off the phone for 30 minutes at a time. She will be told to expect anxiety, but her therapist has taught her a relaxation technique that will help to keep her calm. As she progresses, Emily will increase the number of uncertainties in her life. For example, she might check her email just once a day, stop prevaricating and make decisions in a set amount of time or go to the cinema to break her more predictable routines.

In summary, the routine for Emily's sessions will go something like this:

- Forms are filled in by Emily that will provide a way for the therapist to assess and measure symptoms and monitor progress.
- Emily outlines the biggest problems she's encountered over the past week, something the therapist calls 'agenda setting'.
- The therapist will 'bridge' the previous session with this one by reflecting on positive and negative experiences and perhaps reminding Emily of certain important features regarding her situation.
- Self-help tasks in the form of 'homework' will be negotiated and agreed.

- Emily might be taught new skills that will help challenge or modify her beliefs and thinking patterns so they become more adaptive.
- As the session draws to a close the therapist may ask Emily how she felt the session went, whether she has any questions, concerns or anything she'd like to see changed.

There are a number of YouTube videos on the topic of CBT. Dr Alina Gorgorian provides a short YouTube clip on the topic at <www.youtube.com/watch?v=X8qaJclDaFQ>, and, if you'd like a YouTube introduction to the general topic of CBT, try <www.youtube.com/watch?v=KyluZW23m0U>.

The downside

CBT doesn't suit everyone. It isn't an easy fix and you have to commit yourself to a process that is sometimes challenging and uncomfortable. Some people find the emphasis on logic and structure too cold and feel that something is lacking in not addressing personal histories and emotions. CBT is effective but it does not solve personal problems, and there is no cast-iron guarantee that your worries and anxieties won't return. However, if they do, you'll have the skills to cope with them more effectively.

Counselling

We're all familiar with a basic form of counselling – the kind where one person unburdens their troubles to a sympathetic ear. This simple but very human act can provide relief and comfort and a way to vent stress that might otherwise build up.

These days counselling is big business. There are counselling services for virtually every facet of life, ranging from debt relief to relationships and right through to bereavement. And there are different ways of providing counselling services – face-to-face, group, online and via telephone. Many medical centres, schools and businesses also retain the services of a counsellor. Despite this apparent endorsement of counselling skills there remains scepticism over its true nature and value, some seeing the process as little more than a comforting conversation.

A trained therapeutic counsellor is very different from someone who might use counselling skills as a volunteer or as a part of their job. But there are many different models and variations of counselling, which can make things confusing. What's more, there can be considerable overlap in the variety of techniques used and the language employed. So rather than spend time distinguishing between psychodynamic, Gestalt, transactional analysis and all the other approaches, I'm going to attempt a summary of the broad nature and purpose of counselling in terms of how it might apply to your situation with anxiety.

In general terms your counsellor will want to help you explore the ways your feelings, experiences and behaviour contribute to the issues troubling you. Your discussions will aim to help you find some clarity and possibly resolution in this regard. This will be made all the easier because you know everything you say is completely confidential. Your therapist is not there to judge you nor, for that matter, to advise you or tell you what to do. At some points you may find his or her apparent lack of commitment a little frustrating, but actually this frustration is an echo of your own situation and circumstances. One of the differences between trained therapists and people who are 'just trying to help' is that therapists keep their beliefs, value systems and how they live their lives out of the discussion.

Counselling, then, is a helping approach that encourages you to talk openly and frankly about various aspects of life. These explorations may lead to insights, due in part to the way the therapist revisits key issues and encourages you to examine them from different perspectives. Reframing issues can reduce confusion, lessen tension and lead to clarity.

Does counselling work?

The answer isn't as straightforward as you might think. Various controlled studies suggest that counselling is both popular and effective, but when it comes to questions about its therapeutic nature and how its effects should be measured, things get a bit foggy. For example, some people argue that counselling should be measured as objectively as possible, using standardized scores, while others see assessing the client's feelings as more significant.

To a great extent this reflects some of the tensions that currently exist with regard to how or whether counselling can be compared with something like medicine, where large randomly controlled trials and objective measures form the criteria for success. Counselling may well see its role – and therefore its criteria for success – in very different ways. Rather than setting out to cure a disease process or alleviate its symptoms, the goal for counselling may be for the client to reframe his or her issue and become more accepting of it.

Even so, if you're considering counselling, the evidence from small controlled trials in medical settings suggests that it is as effective as antidepressant medication. The significance for those with anxiety is that these same medications tend to be prescribed for anxiety states.

There are several YouTube clips available on differing approaches to counselling, but I think the introductory teaching video on 'The Counselling Process' is a good starting point. It's targeted at trainee counsellors but provides a good general insight into what you might expect – see <www.youtube.com/watch?v=7qOCCvreTaI>.

Frozen trauma

Therapy doesn't stand still. Even the most established and long-standing therapies are constantly refining, redefining and sometimes blending their approaches with those of others. And every so often a new model of thinking appears. Frozen trauma is an example, a concept and resulting therapy largely established by the American therapist Peter Levine. It is one of the new kids on the therapy block and as such now requires careful study and evaluation as to its effectiveness. I leave it for you to consider, but the following is the gist of it.

Levine suggests that many so-called adult problems and disorders stem from undischarged traumas that tend to be stored up during childhood and become triggered in adult life. As children we have neither the capacity nor the experience to cope with overly stressful experiences. So overpowering are the subsequent emotions they simply can't be accommodated or, in Levine's terms, the energy cannot be fully discharged so it becomes locked in or 'frozen'. According to Levine, people who suffer from anxiety, depression, emotional sensitivity and various other disorders have the shared experience of frozen traumas that become physical responses trapped in the nervous system. Part of the therapeutic approach is to focus on physical sensations that indicate frozen energy is being released.

A few YouTube videos of Dr Levine are available. In this example he uses a slinky to demonstrate his approach – see <www.youtube.com/watch?v=ByalBx85iC8>.

Hypnosis for anxiety

I've included hypnotherapy in this chapter for two reasons. First, I get many questions about its effectiveness, which is no doubt due to the second reason, which is that it's a fairly heavily promoted technique for a range of anxiety-related disorders. As a standalone therapy in its own right I personally find it too narrow in scope to address issues of worry and anxiety, although as an adjunct – one tool among others – it may have its uses.

Hypnotherapy techniques vary somewhat but typically involve a preliminary phase of assessment, rapport-building and dealing with any misconceptions or concerns about hypnosis.

The next phase is along the lines of combining relaxation with the use of some internal focus and imagery – a process often described as hypnotic induction. The treatment phase extends hypnotic induction by using relaxation, imagery and suggestions to facilitate change, or sometimes to access unconscious memories or mechanisms that have a bearing on the problem. Finally, post-hypnotic suggestions are used to reinforce therapy. This is also a time for building belief in change and for establishing self-confidence in the client.

Hypnosis used for symptom relief is different from that used for resolving memories and personal conflicts. Suggestive hypnosis is frequently applied to conditions such as social anxiety and smoking, but also to conditions and disorders that are aggravated by psychological factors. Here we can think of things such as migraine, certain skin complaints and irritable bowel syndrome. This mind-to-body link underpins the approach to

clinical hypnosis. The strong associations we form during a difficult experience, and our emotional reaction to it, may set up a
scenario whereby the same or similar situations are responded to
with some degree of anxiety.

All of which leads me to the question: Does it actually work?
There is some evidence to suggest that hypnosis can help reduce
anxiety, but studies and results to date tend to be underwhelming
in terms of their scope and quality. A systematic review published
in 2009 by the University of York also found little persuasive evidence of the overall effectiveness of hypnosis. This may appear a
gloomy assessment but it simply reflects the situation as it currently stands. We shouldn't write hypnotherapy off, but until we
can establish a clearer understanding of its active components –
that is, what it is that is meant to work – and there are some well-
controlled large clinical trials to support it, hypnosis is probably
best thought of as an option that you may feel is worth trying,
particularly if it forms part of a wider formal treatment approach.

8

Self-help and remedies

If you've just read about cognitive behavioural therapy in the previous chapter, you will have noticed the emphasis placed on structure and homework tasks. In effect, the therapist provided a framework, guidance and support but Emily, the patient, did the taxing work by identifying her beliefs and feelings and setting workable treatment goals. Emily negotiated homework tasks with the therapist, but she had to do them, monitor her progress and use the skills she had acquired to make progress.

This tells us something very important about ourselves, which is that we can be our own very powerful agents of change. Self-help is no cop-out. For it to be effective it requires the same – or possibly higher – levels of motivation than working alongside a therapist. This is one of the reasons it can be helpful to kick-start a self-help programme by working with a therapist – he or she can introduce you to a variety of essential skills, explain their purpose and show you what to do.

Even so these same skills can be self-taught, and so we've reached a point where we're going to look at them in more detail. Some have the added benefit of an emerging research base that points to their effectiveness, others do not.

I can't cover everything and frankly some suggestions, such as dolphin therapy, drinking urine or snake massage, are well outside what most of us regard as acceptable or practicable. So my compromise is to address topics I've specifically and regularly been asked about and some others I feel worthy of consideration and that others too have asked me about.

Mindfulness

There's increasing interest in how this ancient practice can help us identify the signs of anxiety and deal with them better. At one level mindfulness might be considered a form of complementary medicine but some therapists have been incorporating its principles and practices into their approach for years.

Mindfulness is about present-centredness. It is about paying attention to and becoming more aware of our surroundings in the here and now. Taking notice of the present moment is about observing everything but in a way that is free of judgements. When you finish this paragraph, look away for a few moments and take notice of the sounds, smells and sights around you. Can you also notice your thoughts and feelings and the way they move around and change? You've just had your first taste of mindfulness.

This is an approach that doesn't set out to try and fix or change anything, which you may think is a little odd given the emphasis so far on doing just that. This is really about clarity. It's a way of standing back from ourselves so that we can begin to absorb our surroundings and see patterns of thought and even notice how certain thought-streams are tying us up in knots.

Mindfulness can be taught over several sessions, mostly as a class and usually as a means of stress reduction. As a self-help strategy here are some guidelines to get you started. Mindfulness is about accepting things as they are, being observant and fully in the moment and impartial to any thoughts or emotions that come your way. If you've always been a goal-focused person and a finisher of tasks you may find these concepts something of a struggle initially. I urge you to try, however, as the effects are so beneficial.

- So let's keep it real. There's no need to put on crimson robes, light incense sticks and adopt an awkward sitting position from which you'll later have trouble untangling yourself. This is about how you live and what you do. If you're at your work desk, that's how it is.
- A few short moments of mindfulness may be more beneficial than trying to put 30 minutes aside. Tune into one thing first – maybe yourself. Are your hands warm? Is your jaw tight? Then after a few moments let your mind go for a wander, picking up the sounds, sights and smells of things around you. Remember: don't judge, simply notice.

- Remind yourself to become mindful by anchoring it to routines – perhaps during your coffee breaks and over lunch and preferably not at times you're likely to be interrupted.

You can apply these principles to everything from eating to breathing. Here's an example of how to sit mindfully. If it's your first attempt, give yourself five minutes and, if the weather is kind, go outside and enjoy the fresh air. Sit comfortably on an upright chair so that your feet are flat to the ground. Be aware of your posture and don't slouch, which will restrict your breathing. Expect and allow your mind to wander. Allow the thoughts to come and go as they must, and then refocus on the exercise.

- Take a deep breath and close your eyes.
- Take notice of yourself physically. How does the chair feel? How warm are your hands and feet? Continue to breathe slowly and regularly.
- Now focus on your hearing. What sounds can you hear? The drone of passing cars? A clock ticking? Birds? Wind? Creaks, snaps? Don't just tick them off in your mind – try to pay attention to each and listen attentively.
- Your next sense is smell. Maybe the first thing you will be aware of is yourself, your perfume or shampoo perhaps. Rooms are often full of smells – cooking, flowers, scented candles or even cold tea in a cup.
- Return to your body. Now you've been using your senses things may feel a little different. You might be more aware of little tensions in facial muscles, and if they are there you're allowed to relax them.
- Breathing comes next. Although you started by taking a deep breath and tried to maintain steady breathing, your breathing might be slower, steadier and more regular than before. Observe how your breathing utilizes the senses. You can feel your chest and stomach move and you can hear your breathing.
- And that's it. When you've finished, have a yawn and stretch.

So far as its relationship to anxiety is concerned it may be helpful to compare mindfulness to CBT. As you know, CBT is about changing the way we think, so we move from a position of over-estimating threats and underestimating our ability to cope, to one where our thoughts are more reasonable and accurate. Mindfulness is about accepting the present and may also be about fully experiencing the symptoms of anxiety, but by opening up to these experiences and observing them, the nature of anxiety is ultimately seen for what it is – just a reaction. Awareness, in this context, serves an important function because once awareness is applied to an automatic feedback system like anxiety, it disrupts it.

In a YouTube clip, Mark Williams, a professor of clinical psychology, provides an entertaining and helpful explanation of how mindfulness works, who it is for and what its benefits are – see <www.youtube.com/watch?v=wAy_3Ssyqqg>.

An easy meditation technique

This is an extension of mindfulness that includes elements of relaxation. Techniques of relaxation are skills-based, meaning they must be developed to get the best from them. Meditation is similar in the sense that the more you practise, the more you will benefit.

Now, because you are anxious you will tend to focus on issues outside of your own thought processes, so this easy meditation approach may be useful. There is no time schedule but I'd suggest that 15 minutes is the minimum to start feeling some positive effects. Just follow these few notes of guidance, which you may later want to adapt to suit your own purposes.

Prepare for this easy meditation in a quiet environment and one where there are likely to be no distractions. If you feel worried or guilty about taking up time to meditate, or you have a sense of squeezing it in between activities, the timing isn't right. Put it off until you feel enough space and time are available.

Let's begin: I now invite you to step outside of yourself and reflect on your emotions and your body almost as though they are not a part of you. Imagine, however, that they can be influenced by you, the observing you. Get comfortable – sitting or lying down is fine.

- Close your eyes and slowly begin to think about your body.
- What parts of the chair or floor are in contact with your body?

- How heavy does your body feel? What parts of your body are warm or cold? Don't attempt to change anything, just become aware of your body.
- Now breathe as if you were taking a few long, lazy sighs. Each time you breathe out, feel some tension leaving your body. Then continue to breathe in a calm and relaxed fashion. Continue to think about your body and observe the changes.
- When you're ready, allow yourself to observe your emotions. Again, don't try to change anything – just become aware of how you're feeling. Perhaps you feel calm; perhaps you observe worry, anger, negativity or love.
- Accept what you feel, but almost as if you were an outsider looking in, so emotions don't take over. Observe your thoughts and feelings as they drift in and out of focus. They may be rational or irrational; they may be memories, trivia or just nonsense. Allow them all to wash around you and simply observe.
- Try inviting a positive or affirming thought to stay for a while. If it seems it doesn't want to, let it go.
- When you feel ready to finish, slowly open your eyes, take a deep breath and return to the world. Many anxious people find that they struggle against who they are and how they feel. Accepting who you are by allowing yourself to observe your body and your emotions can sometimes provide unforeseen insights.

How relaxation benefits health

The many different forms and techniques of relaxation are well known to have stress-reduction effects. All these are great ways to reduce anxiety. What is less well known are the many other positive effects of relaxation that ward off disease and help to maintain health.

When I refer to relaxation I don't mean reading a book or sitting in front of the television. I'm talking about a skill that needs to be acquired, developed and maintained in order to derive maximum benefit. Properly applied, relaxation decreases the activity of the sympathetic nervous system, lowers blood pressure and reduces heart and breathing rates.

Regular relaxation is also highly beneficial for the immune system. The relationship between mental states and the immune system is something Janice Kiecolt-Glaser has investigated for several years. In one study elderly residents in a retirement home were taught relaxation. After just one month levels of natural killer cells and antibody levels increased.

Relaxation also appears to have a natural beta-blocking effect on the heart. This makes it particularly interesting for people involved in cardiac rehabilitation. Regular relaxation reduces blood pressure and cholesterol and actually improves blood-flow to the heart.

Relief from pain is one of the more significant benefits to derive from relaxation. Various studies have shown that relaxation can lead to reductions in pain medication for chronic back pain, migraine or even pain from diseases such as cancer.

The basic skills of relaxation are not difficult to learn, although it may be easier to learn them from a properly qualified teacher rather than something like a CD or download. Relaxation is an entirely natural process that has no side effects. Considering the health benefits that may be derived from as little as 15 minutes a day, the case to integrate it into your life is compelling.

Using breathing and muscle relaxation to reduce anxiety

I'm sure you've all come across those movie scenes where the upset person is told to breathe slowly and deeply. When you're feeling particularly anxious it's not such a bad idea, but filling your lungs with air a couple of times is really only part of the picture. If you're prone to anxiety it's actually more helpful to practise breathing and get used to proper breathing techniques.

Breathing is such a natural function it may seem a little odd to discover there are such things as effective and ineffective breathing. We could say the same about relaxation, but it's only when you compare what comes naturally with what can be taught and felt that you really start to appreciate the differences. Why not try the breathing technique now?

First, test yourself to see how you breathe. Stand up straight and place one hand on your chest and the other towards the top of your stomach. Now take a deep breath and note which of your hands moves first.

A common problem in people who suffer with anxiety and/or panic is the way they breathe. Typically they breathe using just the upper part of their chest and often in a fairly shallow and sometimes rapid fashion. This alone can give rise to a feeling of constriction. A far better approach is to fill the lungs in much the same way a bottle is filled with fluid – from the bottom to the top. So if during the test you felt your chest hand move first, it's time to make a few changes.

Give yourself a few minutes to practise. Get away from distractions and place your hands back over your chest and stomach areas. This time when you breathe in, try to draw air deep into your body. Don't just push your stomach out – you have to get to a point where your stomach moves first *because of* the way you're breathing. Some people get it first time, others need a bit more practice. Here's the technique.

- Begin by placing the palm of your hand just above the waistline of your stomach. Take four or five deep breaths. Feel your stomach area push out a little when you breathe in and feel it go back when you breathe out.
- Once you've got the idea, feel free to remove your hands or maybe just keep one hand on your stomach. What you'll probably find is that concentrating on breathing quickly becomes a little tedious and thoughts begin to crowd in. You might want to try a slow count to five when you breathe in and again when you exhale.
- Now try combining breathing practice with a little muscular relaxation. Sit or lie down in a relaxed posture and settle your breathing into a nice, regular deep pattern.
- As you continue to breathe, think about your legs. Each time you breathe out, feel a little tension leaving your leg and buttock muscles. Continue breathing and thinking about your legs until your legs feel completely relaxed. Any muscular twitches you feel are quite normal and simply mean your muscles are relaxing.

- Follow the same sequence with your arms, back, stomach, neck and head, before embracing a bodily sensation of relaxation.
- You can maintain this for as long as you wish, but most people find anything between 10 and 20 minutes about right for a daily session. Some people then indulge in a longer session perhaps once a week or after a particularly stressful period.

More on relaxation techniques and training

We all use our everyday techniques to calm down or avoid conflict. I've no idea how many times I've 'bitten my tongue, counted to 10 or taken a deep breath' during times of maximum irritation. Equally, during a stressful – or even not so stressful – day I find it useful to claim a few calm moments. None of these needed to be taught and in fact most came about as a result of trial and error, personal circumstances and opportunities.

We all know that a state of calm can result from taking a walk, exercising, reading a book or even stroking a pet. So while most people know how to wind down, surprisingly few can successfully relax beyond a certain point. I previously stated that learning to relax properly is a skill, and I really mean that. I've yet to come across a therapist who hasn't heard, 'I get all the relaxation I need when I go to bed/drink a beer/watch a movie' but none of these actually equate to the technique of relaxation.

Some people view relaxation as an activity for 'alternative' types – people who light candles around their bath and listen to recordings of whale noises. Pigeonholing isn't useful or accurate and frankly if whale noises work for you, that's fine. The reality, however, is quite different, as elite athletes, sportsmen and sportswomen – in fact anyone who has seriously tried relaxation – will attest. What's more, the range of available techniques means that even the twitchiest of individuals can be accommodated.

The most common relaxation methods include progressive relaxation, autogenic training, deep breathing, meditation, hypnosis, biofeedback, music therapy, aerobic exercise, cognitive approaches and pharmacological methods. Although many others exist I have listed those that, to one degree or another, have been evaluated by research.

Why all this emphasis on relaxation? Relaxation is highly effective – both as a preventative measure and a treatment – for psychological and physical conditions. It is recommended as a primary or adjunct therapy for a huge range of problems, including anxiety-related disorders, anger management, pain, high blood pressure, cardiac health and depression. As a technique it is increasingly being recommended as an everyday routine for support of the immune system and to help with a general sense of psychological and emotional well-being.

In clinical contexts the aim of teaching relaxation is to reduce stress and so prevent the emotional and health problems perceived to result from stress. Therapists teach clients how to recognize, control and modify their physical and mental responses to stressful situations. The most common targets are the reduction of muscular tension, overbreathing, tachycardia and gastrointestinal upsets. To this end relaxation may be used in isolation or in combination with other therapies.

What we know about relaxation approaches is that they work differently with different people in different problem situations. Most methods appear to have the desired effects but some are more acceptable than others, depending on preference. In clinical settings a detailed assessment of the individual will also be undertaken to establish levels of motivation, ability to self-regulate and expectations about what can reasonably be expected.

YouTube offerings for relaxation and meditation are many and varied. You may want to try out a few before you settle on one with which you feel comfortable. Unfortunately some are little more than advertising and others are poorly edited. You also need to feel comfortable with the presentational style because both the voice and pacing can influence your receptiveness and enjoyment. I quite like a clip by Dr Deborah Blair, which lasts for 15 minutes – see <www.youtube.com/watch?v=sqeHYXjWtI0>.

Overcoming anticipatory anxiety

One of the most common features of anxiety is something called anticipatory anxiety. This is where anxiety increases just as a result of thinking about what's on the horizon. One thing we know about this form of advance anxiety is that the reality of the feared event or situation is almost always much less than was feared. Even so, if you are someone who suffers with anticipatory anxiety you may like to try the following exercise.

The first step is to relax your body using your favourite relaxation or meditation exercise. During the exercise you may find yourself feeling uneasy as your levels of anxiety start to creep up. This is perfectly normal, but you should try to counteract these feelings by returning to a relaxed state before proceeding.

1 Start by selecting one of the situations or events that causes you to worry. The first task is for you to imagine that situation without your being in it. You should freeze-frame the situation as though time has stopped and only you have the ability to make it start again. If it helps, imagine the scene on a movie screen or on your television, and let your mind make it as vivid as possible. During this time remember to monitor yourself and to remain relaxed.

2 Remember that you are not in the situation – you are outside and cannot be affected by the things you see. You are actually in charge of everything. To keep your mind focused, try to describe everything you see, all the while staying relaxed.

3 Very slowly, add yourself to the situation but in a way that you can see yourself as easily as you see others. You are the actor/director. Stay focused on your breathing and your relaxation. You can release and press the pause button whenever you wish and you can make things happen in slow motion.

4 Now let the action start until you reach a point where the anxiety kicks in. Freeze everything – including yourself as an actor – at that point. Look at yourself and make adjustments to any part of your posture or expression that says 'anxious'. Think about the parts of the body of you, the actor, that are tense and allow yourself as much time as you need to relax and make adjustments.

5 As the person who is directing, you can make any subtle changes you wish to yourself as the actor, but don't let fantasy take over too much. Think constructively about the little things you'd like

to change and encourage yourself to try out new strategies, even though they might feel challenging.

6 Because you have acted and directed and kept things positive, your experience should be positive. Stay calm and relaxed. As you become less self-conscious about the exercise, you'll find you're able to expand the scenario to a point where you can predict yourself able to cope successfully with unforeseen circumstances, comments or whatever makes you anxious.

Preparation before a stressful or demanding activity is a well-accepted technique in a whole variety of sports or professional activities. The fact that your anxiety might relate to driving a car, walking into a room or hosting some event is no different. The use of positive imagery along with personal talk and encouragement is very effective. So why not give it a try?

Posture

If you're someone who worries a great deal there's a good chance you also look heavy and burdened. The reason for this is that you feel vulnerable, exposed or threatened. As a result, your subconscious is doing its thing by trying to protect you. Physically you may have a tendency to curl inwards when you sit; when you stand your tension may show in hunched or slumped shoulders, a lowered head and curved back. Poor posture has far-reaching consequences for both body and mood.

Sitting, standing and walking correctly can take a little practice if you aren't used to it. It can be helpful to check the mirror to see how you stand normally. Even better, get someone who knows about posture – a physiotherapist, yoga instructor, physical trainer – to offer you some feedback. Is it worth all the effort? 'Yes' is the short answer, and here are some of the reasons.

- In people who are anxious or prone to panic, breathing is often quite shallow and a little rapid.
- A slumped posture increases chest compression – the full capacity of the lungs is underused.

- During stressful moments there is a danger of overbreathing, which leads to chest pressure, light-headedness, tingling and increased heart rate. In some people these bodily sensations may be misinterpreted, leading to panic.

Sitting correctly immediately opens the airways and improves circulation. The importance of an effective circulation, feeding organs and the nervous system with necessary oxygen, should not be underestimated. Very often a few small changes are all that is required.

- In a typical upright chair, ensure your lower back is supported and that you are sitting with your back straight and shoulders back.
- Ensure your body weight is distributed evenly and that your feet are flat to the floor.
- If you can, adjust the height of the seat so that the tops of your legs are parallel to the table you are working with.
- Try not to remain in a static seated position for more than around 30 minutes.

Good posture works wonders with self-confidence. In 2009 a study reported in the *European Journal of Social Psychology* illustrated just how influential posture can be. Volunteer job-applicants were asked to complete their mock application forms adopting a slumped sitting or upright posture. The findings revealed that those who slumped were less effective in listing their perceived strengths and less likely to articulate why they should be considered a good candidate for the post.

In the treatment of anxiety and panic quite a lot of attention is given to posture and correct breathing. I don't think there is a therapeutic approach around that doesn't, in some way, indicate the importance of these components. It's good to develop the habit of checking your posture several times a day. When standing:

- keep your shoulders back but relaxed;
- pull in your stomach to stop your lower back curving inward;
- don't allow your head to droop;

- don't bear weight on one leg;
- keep your legs straight when standing but don't lock your knees.

The simple act of changing your posture and breathing pattern can quickly change your mood. Breathing steadily and smoothly through the nose quickly helps to relax the body and improve mood.

Herbal remedies

Many people choose some form of herbal remedy as a calming or reviving supplement. The following list represents some of the more popular choices. Be aware that many of these remedies are not subject to pharmaceutical controls and may therefore vary in strength and potency. If you are taking prescribed medication you should always consult your doctor before taking herbal or other remedies.

St John's wort (hypericum) The medicinal properties of St John's wort have been known about for centuries. In some people it helps lift low moods and may be especially helpful when anxiety is linked to depression. It still isn't clear how St John's wort works but the action is likely to involve some alteration in the balance of neurotransmitters thought to be involved in anxiety and depression. St John's wort has been exposed to some critical scientific examination. It's probably fair to say that the evidence for its effectiveness is very mixed. Various placebo trials suggest that, at most, its effects may be minimal. There are also side effects, the most common of which are fatigue, increased sensitivity to light, upset bowels and dizziness. It can also react with other drugs and cannot therefore be taken alongside prescribed SSRI antidepressants.

Ginseng Often used as a restorative for flagging levels of energy, ginseng is also taken to induce feelings of relaxation and general well-being. There are various types of ginseng and all sorts of claims as to its effects on a variety of health conditions. It too has side effects. Pregnant women are urged to avoid its use and, somewhat ironically perhaps, it can actually increase levels of agitation, nervousness and insomnia. It also has drug interaction effects so shouldn't, for example, be used by anyone taking medication to thin the blood or affect the heart rhythm.

Oatstraw Among the uses of oatstraw is as a tonic and also to enhance feelings of relaxation. People who stand by its use say it benefits both anxiety and depression. Oatstraw may be taken as a tea and is claimed by some to have additional beneficial properties, such as easing the effects of arthritis and enhancing sexual functioning.

Lemon balm The common garden herb lemon balm is said to increase calmness and even improve memory, according to researchers at Northumbria University in the UK. Lemon balm also has the effect of increasing the activity of acetylcholine, an important chemical messenger linked to memory whose level is reduced in people with Alzheimer's disease. Lemon balm also increases levels of the inhibitory brain chemical gamma-aminobutyric acid, which dampens down anxiety, so it may be useful for such things as exam stress. The suggested daily dose is around 650mg, three times daily.

Chamomile (camomile) I'm partial to a cup of chamomile tea myself. Not only does it taste nice, it's also said to have properties that help reduce anxiety and promote sleep. Unfortunately, the National Institutes of Health in the USA warn that its reputation as a gentle medicinal plant is not entirely warranted, pointing out that many people have allergic reactions after coming into contact with chamomile preparations, a few of which have even been life threatening.

Reishi Sometimes described as the mushroom of immortality, reishi is considered to lower blood pressure, boost energy and promote restful sleep. It has also been used as an immune stimulant by some patients with HIV/AIDS or cancer because a number of its polysaccharides, such as beta glucans, have demonstrated anti-tumour and immunostimulating activities.

Guarana A climbing plant of the maple family, guarana has fruit about the size of a coffee bean that actually contain at least two to three times the amount of caffeine as coffee. Its main purported effects are to increase energy levels and improve the stress response. The extract is found in certain cans of soda. It is also used as an infusion in tea and is also in some herbal slimming pills due to its appetite-suppressing properties. The evidence as to its positive effects is mixed but its side effects are better known. It has been found to interact with certain drugs, such as monoamine oxidase inhibitors, and can increase the risk of bleeding if taken alongside anticoagulants. It is also possible to overdose on guarana – signs include vomiting and stomach cramps.

Yoga

If, like me, you don't know your mountain pose from your fish posture, it's clear yoga has passed you by. But if you'd like to improve your mood and lessen your anxiety naturally, yoga may be just the thing for you.

One thing I do know a little about is gamma-aminobutyric acid (GABA), and this is the key to what we might call the yoga effect. Yoga is said to increase levels of GABA, so to understand its significance it helps to know a thing or two about GABA.

GABA is a naturally occurring substance found in the brain. It is a neurotransmitter that has a specific role in the anxiety response. Its main action is one of inhibiting nerve cells from firing. Low levels of GABA mean high levels of activity between nerve cells, all of which results in the fight-or-flight response associated with stress. Put another way, low levels of GABA lead to high levels of fear.

The effect of benzodiazepine drugs such as diazepam (Valium) is to enhance the action of GABA, which in turn reduces levels of anxiety. Similarly, alcohol is known to enhance the action of GABA within the hypothalamus and sympathetic nervous system. The problem with alcohol is that it also has the effect of reducing natural production of GABA, which can easily lead to dependence on alcohol to maintain a desired emotional state. Although stopping alcohol consumption may be uncomfortable to begin with, the good news is that natural levels of GABA are eventually re-established.

But to get back to yoga, researchers at the Boston University School of Medicine have been reporting interesting findings with yoga for some time. In 2007 they published findings in the *Journal of Alternative and Complementary Medicine*, suggesting that depression and anxiety could be relieved through the practice of yoga. They compared levels of GABA in volunteers prior to and after one hour of yoga and compared the results with another group of volunteers who sat and read for the same amount of time. An increase of 27 per cent in GABA was observed in volunteers who undertook yoga.

More recently the researchers compared yoga with walking and other forms of exercise. Once again they found that yoga had a greater positive effect. The conclusion is that yoga postures seem to stimulate specific areas of the brain associated with GABA production. Quite how the mechanism works and how sustainable the effects are have yet to be fathomed. Still, as an alternative or possibly even a supplement to drugs, it clearly appears to have merit for further investigation. Meanwhile there's nothing stopping any of us getting involved in this natural and useful form of exercise and relaxation.

A YouTube video by Sue Tupling focuses on simple and practicable techniques for use by people experiencing anxiety – see <www.youtube.com/watch?v=c8dDFlVMfiw>.

Writing

I suspect that comparatively few people would add writing about emotional experiences to their list of self-help treatments for anxiety. Well, for the past 20 years or so a variety of studies have pointed to significant physical and mental health improvements when people use writing as a therapeutic tool.

Dr James W. Pennebaker, a professor of psychology at the University of Texas, is one of the leading figures in the development of the method. Pennebaker and his colleagues first noticed that many of the scales devised to measure the effects of stress on people's health tended to focus on socially acceptable issues – death of a spouse, loss of a job – and avoided more sensitive areas such as rape, being the victim of violence, causing the death of others and so on. It also became clear that people who kept silent about personal traumas were significantly more likely to suffer adverse health effects. This prompted Pennebaker to test whether writing, as a form of disclosure, might be beneficial.

Initial research, conducted by Pennebaker and Beale in 1986, was promising. People were simply asked to write about a trauma for 15 minutes a day over a period of four days. They discovered that the simple act of writing appeared to tap into deep personal emotions, which in turn resulted in a reduction in visits to the doctor, reduced self-medication and a positive evaluation of the writing experience.

Since then a whole series of investigations have been conducted, producing a variety of findings. One study found that writing or talking about emotions has a positive influence on immune function and reduces blood pressure. A second suggested that writing by hand seems to be more beneficial than typing, possibly because the act of writing is slower and encourages deeper reflection.

To date there appears to be no consensus as to whether an optimal time exists after trauma for expressive writing to be most effective. Some have suggested therapy within a 72-hour window of trauma, but studies suggest this may do more harm than good.

The reasons why expressive writing appears to have beneficial effects for people who worry also remain unclear. No single reason explains its effectiveness but some possible ideas have been put forward. One suggestion is that people are more likely to inhibit thoughts and feelings viewed as socially threatening. It follows that offering a method that enables disclosure may result in health benefits.

Simply documenting the details of a trauma in a detached fashion does not lead to any improvement – an essential component is emotional engagement. Another possible explanation comes from the principles of learned association: repeated exposure to emotional stimuli will eventually break the link between an event and a person's emotional reaction to it. So writing provides the vehicle through which these negative ties might be broken.

Solving problems to overcome worries

In Chapter 1 I pointed out that a major reason you worry is that you dislike uncertainty. In fact I was talking to my wife about this section, what I might put in or leave out and what examples we might draw on from our own experiences to illustrate certain points. I was quickly reminded of several potential entries, but for our purposes just one should do!

It was our wedding anniversary. We booked ourselves a night away somewhere and our kind friends volunteered to look after our then still very young daughter. In principle it was great. Our friends had a daughter the same age and they got on very well together. But it was also the first time we'd been separated from our daughter overnight. The moment we set off the 'What ifs' began. Then we'd check ourselves, realizing it was pointless to fret. We had a nice break but it was frequently peppered with the language of worry, like 'I wonder if?' and 'Should we?' and 'Do you think?'

Being a psychologist, psychiatrist or psychoanalyst doesn't detach you from the emotions of the human race – if anything it probably sharpens them. Our imaginations can still fill the gaps that uncertainty provides and we, like you, can still wrestle with various scenarios and possible outcomes. In generating these problems we fuel the uncertainties and in turn become more anxious. The fact that we are burning so much mental fuel may feel like we are problem-solving, but what we are actually doing is very different.

Incidentally, when we got home we discovered a very happy daughter who apparently hadn't really noticed we'd gone. Thus emboldened, we took another leave of absence some weeks later. When we returned we discovered our daughter had been miserable – maybe a misery. But whether we had worried or not would not have made a jot of difference to the outcome.

Worrying is a process that focuses on things that haven't happened and may never happen. Problem-solving focuses on difficulties at hand by considering practicable and achievable solutions. The way to do this is as follows:

- Define the problem as solvable or unsolvable. A solvable worry might be, 'Can't agree with my partner whether we go to his or my parents for Christmas'. An unsolvable problem is more on the lines of 'I might have an accident'. We can do something with the solvable!
- List the possible solutions – for example, go with a flick of a coin; talk with your partner as to why it's more important to see her parents this year (there may be a good reason); see both sets of parents but over a shorter period.

- Remove solutions that seem less practicable or desirable and list the remainder in order of preference.
- Consider the top two or three in terms of their benefits and limitations.
- Agree a compromise. In problems where agreements can't be reached, only a compromise can go some way in giving you both a voice, meeting some of your needs and ensuring there are no winners or losers.

Exercise

If something could be invented that would genuinely and significantly reduce your risk of dementia, heart disease, anxiety, depression, diabetes and early death, you'd surely want it. Well, it's already here – it's free, safe, natural and it's called exercise.

Regular exercise has some interesting effects. Experiments reported in the *Journal of Neuroscience* reveal that regular exercise has the effect of leading to a spike in the activity of GABA. You may recall from Chapter 2 that GABA is a neurotransmitter that acts like a brake for neural activity. It reduces anxiety – the more we have of it, the greater our ability to calm those excitable neurons, and the calmer we feel.

There may be other neurological benefits, as researchers from the School of Public Health at the University of Maryland discovered when they compared the effects of exercise with quiet rest. Using a set of photographs designed to elicit a range of emotions, researchers found that anxiety levels of volunteers who rested climbed up around 20 minutes later. By contrast, those volunteers who exercised maintained reduced anxiety levels.

I'm no paragon of virtue when it comes to exercise. I even joined a fitness club once, only to drop out before my introductory period had lapsed. For various reasons it didn't work for me, so I now do other things that fit more easily into my lifestyle. It's not hard to be active, and what really counts is that you're doing things regularly and at a level of intensity that puts up your heart rate. The correct level of intensity would put you in a situation where you can still talk but you may need to catch your breath from time to time. Activities such as cycling, digging, brisk walking and swimming would count, but things like housework and shopping wouldn't because they tend not to raise the heart rate for long enough.

Recommended physical activity levels are easily achievable:

- age 5–18: 60 minutes per day;
- age 19 upwards: 150 minutes per week.

So for most adults a commitment to just over two hours of moderate intensity exercise per week is enough to bring about improvements in mental and physical health.

I mentioned my own failure with a fitness club for a reason, and that is because I fell into that age-old trap of allowing enthusiasm to run ahead of me. It all seemed so easy at first, but the fact that I had to travel across town and back began to nibble away at my motivation, as did finding the extra oomph after the working day. Slowly but surely it was easy to find excuses not to bother.

As someone who's looking towards the back end of my fifties I tend to cluster various activities. I meet a friend for what we loosely call golf; my dog takes me for long walks; I do a good amount of DIY and gardening; if the weather is decent I'll cycle a few miles to a coffee shop. I find building a treat into some activities gives me an incentive. In other words, for me it's about building exercise into my daily life in such a way that I don't even think of it as exercise.

You might also want to consider combining hobbies with activities. For example, you could dust off that camera and take it with you on a walk, or maybe use a sketch pad. If you like to cook, why not go foraging for wild mushrooms, herbs and berries? If you think others would be interested in what you're doing, you could start a blog. And what about trying out something that will get you into the fresh air – bird watching, fishing, community volunteering, sailing or painting the fence? Not everything has to be a long-term commitment, but if you're not used to considering the options, you may need to make a list just to get started.

9

Cultivating calm and confidence

Right now, reading this book, you are fine. Your troubles, as we've explored, stem from your past as well as concerns over the future. The more you focus on the future the more is the likelihood that you will worry. I won't pretend that it's easy to let go of the things that make you who you are, but your life is already plagued by worry and anxiety so you must surely try. Therefore resolve to:

- let go of old resentments;
- let go of the painful memories;
- let go of trying to predict the future;
- let go of your physical tensions;
- let go of the guardedness, the stiffness and vigilance that drain you – enjoy bending with the breeze.

Let's explore these first two bullet points a little further. Painful memories and resentments often work together, and while they can certainly result from recent experiences, I think we all know just how far back they can stretch. Resentments are emotionally taxing and quite destructive. Invariably the focus is some form of injustice or unfairness with which we feel burdened, but the effect is that we are unwilling or unable to let it go, perhaps in misjudged belief that our quest to be right will somehow culminate in a resolution of these same hurtful emotions.

We've already explored just how powerful your own set of beliefs can be and how it can affect your behaviour. Many people with anxiety and depression – depression tends to be a close friend of anxiety – experience a lot of anger and resentment but sometimes are unable to articulate why.

It's important to see resentments and painful memories for what they are; that is, they're in the past, and while they may still be affecting you, you cannot change the past. Resentment is a powerful emotion that leads people astray. It distorts thinking and puts a bias towards the negative, which only encourages worry and anxiety.

We need therefore to turn this situation around. Next time you find yourself ruminating, don't try to suppress your thoughts. If you do you'll find they only rebound (do you remember the monkey in Chapter 1?), and you'll ruminate even more. Work instead with some of the techniques I've identified in this book. Allow the thoughts to arise but stand back from them as if they're nothing to do with you. It's like picking up a pebble from the beach: you could try examining it from different angles, then when you're done, put it back down. This approach derives from a treatment method called acceptance and commitment therapy (ACT). The principles, as you may have guessed, are rooted in mindfulness.

Positive and negative feelings influence us in very different ways but, curiously, negative feelings can feel like an asset, so we need to be aware of this. For example, it's easier to be critical, to spot mistakes, to become more focused and more detailed when negative feelings dominate, but the key word here is negative. Positive feelings are altogether different. They help us feel expansive, to come up with new ideas and possibilities and consider opportunities rather than problems. So how do we go about moving from one state of affairs to another?

In many ways this whole book is about moving towards a state of calm and confidence, but I don't want you to be in a situation in which you're solemnly reading its contents – perhaps even identifying with the issues – but still not forming the connection that this is about you and for you. Has that struck a chord?

Mindset

I didn't mean to be unsympathetic just then, but I know just how difficult it can be to change a mindset. Worry and anxiety tend to come with something of a fixed mindset. You must believe you have it within you to change or your stubbornness, your fixed mindset, will prevent you from achieving your goals.

Carol S. Dweck, a psychologist, maintains that people with a fixed mindset are overly focused on performance goals and on avoiding failure. When they achieve these goals they feel validated but can still feel anxious because it means they have to work as hard or harder to maintain the status quo. When these often self-imposed standards can't be met, they feel hopeless and helpless.

Carol Dweck contrasts this with a growth mindset, in which people remain open to new ideas, are willing to take a risk on trying something new and don't get hung up on issues like winning or losing, or passing or failing.

One thing we can say about fixed-mindset folk is that they tend to be persistent. When confronted by a problem, they typically keep repeating the same behaviour while hoping for a different outcome. They resist trying new ideas and as a result all the negative emotions they carry just follow them around.

One of the techniques Dweck uses to shift the bias towards a growth mindset is to teach people about brain function. We all know we have at least the potential to change, and the same is true of our brains. Using our mind to change our brain isn't far-fetched, and there are plenty of examples to prove the point.

Let's imagine you're a brain – indulge me for a moment. As you go about your business, a worry comes your way so you fire up a few neurons to respond. But this and other worries go on and on, so you think: 'Hang on – this must be really important; I'd better commit more resources to it', and so you fire up a few more neurons and you start to make more robust and stable connections. Before too long you've established a nice neural structure for worry. All right: you can stop being a brain now.

As the Canadian psychologist Donald Olding Hebb once put it: 'Neurons that fire together, wire together'. This tells us something about how we can exert a positive influence over our own brains. Carol Dweck uses this neuroscience knowledge to teach people to learn or practise something new so as to develop their brains in new directions. There's nothing complicated about it, but it does require you to acknowledge that your mindset may have blocked you from getting what you want or where you want to be. The next step is thinking what you could do differently to achieve these goals, rather than repeating the same things over and over and getting nowhere.

Fixed mindsets sound more concrete than they actually are. The fact is, the brain is like any other muscle, and the more you use it and test it and try out new things, the better it will perform.

The neuropsychologist Rick Hanson says that people who routinely relax have improved gene expression, which helps calm stress reactions. You'll also be pleased to note that all the relaxation and mindfulness you'll be undertaking has brain benefits in the form of thicker layers of neurons of the pre-frontal cortex. Mindful activity boosts left pre-frontal cortex activity, which helps to suppress negative emotions and reduces activation of the amygdala – what Hanson refers to as the 'alarm bell of the brain'.

Reduced to its basics we can say that the human condition is a product of genes and the environment. We know we have a certain level of control over our environment, but it is often assumed we have no control over our brain or our genes. I've discussed the brain, but in any attempt to beat anxiety it's worth knowing that some genes are like switches – we can in fact switch them on and off.

Unfortunately our full understanding of genes in relation to anxiety remains a bit sketchy, so the production of a tablet to target and switch off the excesses of anxiety lies a few years off. Anxiety, depression and other mood disorders are known to have a genetic component. Various proteins surround and stick to DNA, and part of the role of these proteins and chemicals is to switch genes on and off.

Factors such as diet are known to have a significant role in switching genes on and off. The implication for anyone with a genetic predisposition towards anxiety and depression is that by balancing environmental influences, such as diet and other lifestyle issues, protective genes can be switched on while others can be switched off. Examples are foods rich in complex carbohydrates, such as rice, corn, barley, peas and lentils. Complex carbohydrates increase the amount of serotonin in the brain, whereas simple carbohydrates do not – simple carbohydrates are found in such foods as sugar, cakes, jams, biscuits and honey and packet cereals.

Of course if it was down to switching to salads, rice and pulses and getting out the rowing machine, everyone's troubles would quickly dissipate. Even so, it does rather depend on the depth of the problem. You may find you achieve complete relief by making changes to your diet and lifestyle, or you may feel just a little better.

So why the differences? Some of the more obvious reasons relate to whether you're male or female. Women, for example, have the burden of having naturally higher levels of stress hormones, while testosterone in men appears to protect against stress.

Early life experiences also appear to have significant effects on the sympathetic nervous system, which can affect levels of sensitivity later and for the whole of life. We are unable to reverse-engineer our early life experiences, but we do have it within our gift to modify their effects.

Our bodies don't discriminate between physical and psychological stress. Stress hormones are as likely to be produced in response to thirst, food additives, caffeine and viral infections as they are to negative emotions. Likewise, a noisy, hot, polluted environment feeds the stress response. Even mild dehydration can affect mood, so drink plenty of water during the day. Alcohol, recreational drugs and cigarettes all have negative effects, although at the time they may feel as though they're alleviating anxiety or low moods.

Resilience

I want to wrap up this section by considering an aspect of the human condition that enables us to bounce back from adversity, grow stronger from negative experiences and prepares us to cope with unforeseen challenges. We call it resilience.

Thomas Edison once said: 'I haven't failed. I have identified 10,000 ways this doesn't work.' You may consider resilience as one of those character traits certain lucky people are born with, but I'm here to tell you that resilience is a skill we can all learn and profit from. With greater resilience comes:

- confidence, emotional stability and a belief that challenges are manageable;
- energy;
- openness to new ideas and experiences;
- more rapid resolution to stress and greater likelihood of calmness;

- generalization – that is, if we develop resilience in just one aspect of life, its effects tend to spread to others.

All right, you want some of this resilience stuff, but let me remind you that you've already got some reserves. Like all of us, you must have experienced setbacks and challenges and yet here you are. My point is that resilience isn't about being non-stick-coated and neither is it about happiness, although that may be a useful spin-off. It's really about coping, but sometimes in different and more adaptive ways than you might be used to.

The way you go about developing resilience is actually a very personal thing. I can offer a few suggestions but what might work for me may mean nothing to you. However, much of what builds resilience is, in some way or another, spread about this book, and that explains why some of the following may look a little familiar.

Problems fall into two camps, namely those that can be solved and those that can't. Life circumstances aren't always pleasant but your objective must be to change how you interpret and respond to them.

Make decisions rather than prevaricate. The more you do nothing the more you create a vacuum into which worry and anxiety will spill. You can't detach from life and wish it wasn't happening. We all make wrong decisions, but if you stand back just in case you do, things will only get worse. Taking some form of action will nearly always improve your perspective on a situation, even if it subsequently means that a different course of action could be more effective.

If you're part of a close family you're fortunate, because this is a key factor in building resilience. Caring and supportive relationships that provide trust, reassurance and encouragement are essential ingredients in developing resilience. Feeling able to ask for help and advice is often easier with people we love and respect.

Not everyone is in this position and not all families are the same, but cultivating friendships and accepting help if and when it is offered are equally important. On this point, you will find that if you offer your services to others, the sense of achievement can be tremendous. Apart from providing them with practical and emotional support you'll probably learn things about yourself.

Try some of the techniques outlined in this book – relaxation, breathing, mindfulness, yoga, exercise all support resilience.

Visualize what you want and set goals to achieve it. Small steps towards meeting your goals are better than doing nothing and feeling fearful – break a big task into smaller achievable steps. Be optimistic and try to accomplish those tasks you have set for yourself.

Be flexible – new approaches may bring with them strong emotions. Give yourself permission to experience these emotions but also learn times when it is best to avoid them. Stepping back to regroup or relax can be just as important as moving forward.

Be experimental – rule in things that work for you and rule out things that don't. As previously mentioned, this is a personal journey. There will be stops and starts, obstructions, smooth paths and rough tracks, but to get to where you want to be this is a route you'll need to take.

10

Assertion

We're moving towards the end of the book, but there's one final important topic we should cover – assertion. In many self-help books about anxiety the issue of assertion is given little more than a passing nod. Yet psychologists like myself know that anxiety, depression, self-worth and self-esteem are intimately related and probably deserve a much higher profile than they are sometimes given. Over the years many of the questions to come my way are from people who feel they have no particular right to an opinion and are often treated like doormats because too much of their time is spent trying to please others or avoid conflict.

A part of assertiveness is the ability to stand up for ourselves and to say how we feel when we need to. This includes:

- expressing how you feel;
- being able to say 'no' without feeling guilty or worried;
- getting what you want rather than always giving in to the needs of others;
- taking action rather than worrying.

As you may already be painfully aware, there's a very strong relationship between worry, anxiety and lack of assertion, particularly so if you find social situations taxing. The most common reason for lack of assertion is fear of the consequences. Typically these involve fearing that others will think you're being selfish or that you may cause some upset or aggressive outburst that you'll then have to cope with. But then if you feel anxious, you already know you're unlikely to be assertive in the first place.

One thing to point out at this stage is that you probably use assertive behaviour without even realizing it. All I'm going to suggest is that you extend this to include new situations and people.

If you're underassertive your behaviour is likely to fall into one of two categories: either you get so worried about what others might think of you that you allow yourself to be walked over; or you're so concerned not to allow this to happen that you send 'keep your distance' signals and appear aloof and unapproachable.

Between these extremes is assertiveness behaviour. Think of assertion as a more appropriate form of behaviour that allows you to stand up for your own rights, resist manipulation and cope with criticism without feeling overwhelming anxiety and without violating the rights of others.

Why assertion matters

Assertiveness is a real boost to self-confidence and will have an immediate and positive effect on anxiety, but you do need some level of self-belief that you can be effective. Not all encounters will necessarily change in the direction you might wish, but your own sense of satisfaction will increase in the knowledge that many will, and no one has been damaged in the process. You'll also quickly discover that your initial anxiety will quickly dissipate, and the more you practise the easier it gets and the more confident you'll become.

Being assertive doesn't mean you have to take on every situation or social encounter as though it's a battle to be won. Moreover the range of situations and events included under the category of 'assertion' might surprise you. I've already mentioned that you're being assertive without knowing it. For example, just thanking someone is an act of assertion; so is admitting you've forgotten someone's name; or that you've forgotten to do something. Apologizing when you are clearly at fault, or making moves to smooth over a previously tense encounter, are yet more examples of assertive behaviour.

So the chances are that you use some or all of these social skills regularly. However, it's probably also true that you use them in situations you don't find threatening, difficult or have had to think about. In situations that are more demanding, anxiety reduces confidence, increases tension and acts like a form of self-sabotage.

Have a look at this example of anxiety-driven talk. Anxiety can easily become self-destructive due to the inner talk that precedes the things we say.

At a sales meeting the manager asks staff why a particular product isn't selling very well. A silence descends. Robert is regarded as the quiet newcomer but on this topic he has a few specific ideas. Sensing an opportunity he hesitantly says, 'Look, I know I'm new here and my opinion probably doesn't really count, but . . .' Just then another member of staff previously lost in thought interrupts Robert to put forward his own ideas. Robert meanwhile quietly backs down.

In this scenario a couple of things have occurred. First, Robert may *appear* to have asserted himself by speaking up, but he also sent a few very loaded messages about himself or rather the way he regards himself. He says: 'What I'm about to say to you probably has little relevance or importance.' His message also says: 'I'm used to being disregarded and overlooked so maybe you should treat my opinions with caution.' How might a more assertive Robert have managed the situation?

An obvious first step would be for Robert to stop prefacing his suggestions with confidence-undermining comments. He could also use non-verbal behaviour as a way of underpinning what he's saying as something worth listening to, by:

- sitting upright in a relaxed posture;
- speaking in a steady, measured fashion;
- never looking beaten by comments or criticism;
- never scowling, looking threatening or looking angry;
- actively listening to others rather than his own inner voice of doubt.

Basic assertion also requires you to stand up for your own rights, but if you're unused to this you may either back down entirely or blurt something out that's inappropriate. So it's handy to arm yourself with one or two stock phrases that are acceptable and non-aggressive. When Robert was overtalked he might have said: 'Excuse me – I'd just like to finish what I was saying.' In the vast majority of cases the other person will accept that he or she has made a social gaffe, give way and possibly say sorry.

Behaving assertively means holding a line between non-assertion and aggression. This isn't always easy, especially if the other person is being aggressive or asserting power or authority over you.

But most social encounters are based on a system of mutual benefit. For example, if someone asks you to swap shifts, you have a few possible choices:

* you could comply, even though you don't want to swap;
* you could say: 'No thanks';
* you could say you'll get back and then use the time to think about whether this is what you want, or to work out some alternatives;
* you could agree, but only if the other person agrees to do something for you.

All these are possibilities and all, except the first, are examples of assertion. Here are some more examples of assertion that link to an opinion.

* Actually, I prefer the blue dress (*because it matches those shoes*).
* I'll have a white wine, please (*I find mulled wine too strong*).
* That's a good idea (*I still prefer the first so let's weigh up the benefits of both*).

The first example allows the other person to make a choice. You've asserted an opinion about the dress and given your reasons. The second example asserts a strength of opinion that makes it quite clear you won't be drinking mulled wine (and I don't blame you – I don't like it either). The third example communicates your willingness to change your view if the argument is strong enough in the opposite direction.

So far we've established what assertiveness is, that it is very different from aggressive behaviour and that it occurs in a whole variety of situations. Now let's look at some ways to improve your assertiveness by first considering the ground rules of assertion and comparing yourself against them. In 1975 a book was published that even today provides the basis for most assertiveness training. *When I Say No, I Feel Guilty* was written by the psychologist Manuel J. Smith, who outlined a ten-point 'Bill of Assertive Rights' that states:

- You have the right to judge your own behaviour, thoughts and emotions, and to take responsibility for their initiation and consequences upon yourself.
- You have the right to offer no reasons or excuses for justifying your behaviour.
- You have the right to judge if you are responsible for finding solutions to other people's problems.
- You have the right to change your mind.
- You have the right to make mistakes – and be responsible for them.
- You have the right to say, 'I don't know'.
- You have the right to be independent of the goodwill of others before coping with them.
- You have the right to be illogical in making decisions.
- You have the right to say, 'I don't understand'.
- You have the right to say, 'I don't care'.

Assertiveness techniques

I want to introduce you to three assertiveness techniques that you can practise in situations in which you feel comfortable, and then extend them to situations in which your worry and anxiety are more pronounced.

The broken record

This technique is designed to protect you from direct manipulation or the indifference of others. For example:

BOSS: I'm looking for a volunteer to run career day.

YOU: I'm sorry, I'm up to my neck in work and I just don't have the time.

BOSS: I might be able to pay you for the extra work.

YOU: I'd like to help but really I'm too busy to take on extra work.

BOSS: Look, I hate to ask, but there's nobody else available.

YOU: I'm not available either, sorry. As I say, I'm up to my neck in work.

The broken record technique requires you to stand your ground politely but firmly and to repeat a central message until the person gets it.

Fogging

Fogging is a way of accepting criticism without its getting to you or escalating into conflict. In a sense, you become the fog. We may not like fog but no matter how much we huff and puff, or hit out at it, it quickly becomes clear the fog won't hit back and it's pointless trying to make it. Fogging takes away the power of provocation, often by agreeing with the person who is goading you. For example:

JACK: Tell me, how is it I work just as hard as you but you always seem to get the recognition?
JANE: You do work hard, that's true.
JACK: But how come you're the golden girl and I'm basically ignored?
JANE: You're right, it's not good to feel unappreciated.

These may appear submissive statements but your technique of fogging denies the other person the outcome he or she is seeking, whether this is confrontation, intimidation or disempowerment. It requires self-control, and while you may feel anxious during the exchange, such situations can't be sustained or escalate without your contribution.

Describe, Express, Specify, Consequences (DESC)

This is something that improves with time and practice but you could try the technique at home or in situations in which you feel safer or more comfortable. Perhaps start with something familiar and then extend it to other circumstances.

> *House mates:* Your music is way too loud (**Describe**). I'm trying to do these accounts for a client and I'm in danger of making mistakes (**Express** your feelings). You don't have to turn it off, just down, or wear some earphones (**Specify** your requirements). When I'm done, we can go out for a drink (**Consequences**).

You need to give a little thought to the Consequences aspect. People tend to respond more favourably to positive inducements or praise than they do to threats or ultimatums.

> *At work:* This is the third time I've asked you to correct this work (**Describe**). It's putting me behind schedule and I'm not at all satisfied (**Express** your feelings). Make the necessary corrections now please and get them to me within the hour (**Specify** your requirements). If this happens again, we'll have to discuss your performance more formally (**Consequences**).

Let's try to summarize all this. First and foremost, you are unique and no matter what I say or suggest there will always be lines in the sand you won't cross, times you will remain quiet when perhaps you shouldn't and there are things you won't do when perhaps you should. In this regard you're no different from me or anyone else. Assertion is about trying to restore some balance into your life and in so doing, reduce the amount of worry and anxiety you experience. The Bill of Assertive Rights is a good reference point for us all and I also suggest these few dos and don'ts.

Don't:

- base your life around trying to win the approval of others;
- put everyone else before yourself;
- worry about saying 'no';
- make excuses or apologize for being the person you are;
- apologize when it isn't your fault.

Do:

- remember you always have a choice;
- say 'yes' and 'no' with conviction;
- give yourself credit where it's due and learn to recognize situations in which you've been successful;
- understand that in taking this on board, you can't please all the people all the time – but then you never could.

11

Moving forwards

We've covered a great deal of ground – examined the nature of worry and anxiety and considered the issues that make things worse and better. I said at the outset that much of what is contained in this book comes from questions I've been asked over time, so I hope I've managed to answer some of these to your satisfaction.

Even so you may now be wondering whether your symptoms are better treated professionally or whether self-help is an appropriate option.

To establish whether you might benefit from professional treatment, let's start by focusing on the issue(s) affecting you. Broadly, they are likely to have involved one or more of the following for the past six months:

- You've been feeling extreme unease and apprehension about various situations and experiences.
- Despite knowing that your sensations are inhibiting your life, you're unable to reassure yourself.
- You've felt restless, tense, irritable and frequently tired.
- You've had one or more episodes of extreme fear or panic and you now have ongoing concerns that this will happen again and get worse.
- In some situations you feel trapped or extremely vulnerable. As a result you try to avoid these situations, which has resulted in some limitations on your behaviour.

If any one or more of these statements looks familiar, the chances are you would benefit from therapy. But the time frame is important. Everyone is entitled to periods of anxiety or concerns and many of these will result from normal and everyday situations. In such cases a little relaxation and some return to a reasonable work–life balance should help resolve the situation. However, if your symptoms have been going on for weeks or months the chances that they will be relieved without some form of intervention are reduced.

I mentioned previously that symptoms of anxiety can sometimes result from physical problems. For this reason your first port of call should be your family doctor, who may well run some blood tests. If physical symptoms can be discounted, it may be time for psychological therapy – which may (or may not) be combined with some form of medication.

And finally:

- don't be too harsh on yourself if things aren't going as well as you'd hoped. You may not have the same sort or degree of support, encouragement or personal resources others have. This is not a race to get better or to improve – there are no time limits;
- try to get exercise, sleep, maintain a healthy diet – if your body is healthy and your mind is rested, you will cope so much better;
- learn to relax and become mindful of your surroundings;
- take charge of your life and assert your rights as an individual;
- nurture friendships with those who offer encouragement and support;
- regularly review your accomplishments and qualities;
- accept that you are a good person with good qualities who is not perfect (who is?), and that you're doing well.

The more worry and anxiety intrude into and cause upset to our lives, the greater the need to do something about it. I believe there are many effective options open to us in this regard. My hope is that you take my suggestions on board, take them to heart and gain some relief. Have faith. Don't give up. Believe in yourself.

Useful addresses

British Association for Behavioural and Cognitive Psychotherapy
Imperial House
Hornby Street
Bury
Lancs BL9 5BN
Tel.: 0161 705 4304
Website: www.babcp.com

British Association for Counselling and Psychotherapy
BACP House
15 St John's Business Park
Lutterworth
Leics LE17 4HB
Tel.: 01455 883300 (general enquiries)
Website: www.bacp.co.uk

British Psychoanalytic Council
Suite 7, 19–23 Wedmore Street
London N19 4RU
Tel.: 020 7561 9240
Website: www.psychoanalytic-council.org

British Psychological Society
St Andrews House
48 Princess Road East
Leicester LE1 7DR
Tel.: 0116 254 9568
Website: www.bps.org.uk

British Wheel of Yoga
25 Jermyn Street
Sleaford
Lincs NG34 7RU
Tel.: 01529 306851
Website: www.bwy.org.uk

Mind
15–19 Broadway
Stratford
London E15 4BQ
Tel.: 020 8519 2122 (general); 0300 123 3393 (Mind Infoline)
Website: www.mind.org.uk

Mind Cymru
Third Floor, Quebec House
Castlebridge
5–19 Cowbridge Road East
Cardiff CF11 9AB
Tel.: 029 2039 5123
Website: www.mind.org.uk

Relate
Tel.: 0300 100 1234
Website: www.relate.org.uk

UK Council for Psychotherapy
Second Floor, Edward House
2 Wakley Street
London EC1V 7LT
Tel.: 020 7014 9955
Website: www.ukcp.org.uk

References

Anxiety Disorders Association of America, 'Anxiety in the Elderly' (undated), <www.adaa.org/GettingHelp/AnxietyDisorders/Elderly.asp>. Note: this article has been deleted but can be retrieved by entering the given URL on the Internet Archive's 'Wayback Machine' website (accessed March 2014).

Baer, J. C., Kim, M. and Wilkenfeld, B., 'Is it Generalized Anxiety Disorder or Poverty? An Examination of Poor Mothers and Their Children'. *Child and Adolescent Social Work Journal* 29(4), 2012.

Barsky, Arthur J., *Worried Sick: Our Troubled Quest for Wellness*, Boston: Little, Brown, 1988.

Baumrind, D., 'The Influence of Parenting Style on Adolescent Competence and Substance Use'. *Journal of Early Adolescence* 11(1), 1991, pp. 56–95.

Bilkei-Gorzo, A., Erk, S., Schürmann, B. et al., 'Dynorphins Regulate Fear Memory: from Mice to Men'. *The Journal of Neuroscience* 32(27), 2012, pp. 9335–43.

Brinol, P., Petty, R. E. and Wagner, B., 'Body Posture Effects on Self-Evaluation: A Self-Validation Approach'. *European Journal of Social Psychology* 39(6), 2009, pp. 1053–64.

Coplan, J., Hodulik, S., Mathew, S. J. et al., 'The Relationship Between Intelligence and Anxiety: An Association with Subcortical White Matter Metabolism'. *Frontiers in Evolutionary Neuroscience* 3(8), 2012.

Eluvathingal, T. J., Chugani, H. T., Behen, M. E. et al., 'Abnormal Brain Connectivity in Children after Early Severe Socioemotional Deprivation: A Diffusion Tensor Imaging Study'. *Pediatrics* 117(6), 2006, pp. 2093–2100.

Freudenberger, Herbert J. and Richelson, Geraldine, *Burn Out: The High Cost of High Achievement. What it is – and How to Survive it*, Garden City, NY: Anchor Press, 1980.

Fry, P. S., 'Perfectionism and Other Related Trait Measures as Predictors of Mortality in Diabetic Older Adults: A Six-and-a-Half-Year Longitudinal Study'. *Journal of Health Psychology* 16(7), 2011, pp. 1058–70.

Hofman, S. G., Moscovitch, D. A., Litz, B. T., Kim, H. J., Davis, L. L. and Pizzagalli, D. A., 'The Worried Mind: Autonomic and Prefrontal Activation During Worrying'. *Emotion* 5(4), 2005, pp. 464–75.

Johnson, F. A., 'Psychotherapy of the Elderly Anxious Patient', in C. Salzman and B. D. Lebowitz (eds), *Anxiety in the Elderly: Treatment and Research*, New York: Springer, 1991, pp. 215–48.

Kagan, J. and Arcus, D., 'The Neurodevelopmental Origins of Behavioural Inhibition', 1994. Symposium paper presented at the Annual Meeting of the American Psychiatric Association, Philadelphia, PA.

Kiecolt-Glaser, J. K., Glaser, R., Gravenstein, S., Malarkey, W. B. and Sheridan, J., 'Chronic Stress Alters the Immune Response to Influenza Virus Vaccine in Older Adults'. *Proceedings of the National Academy of Sciences of the United States of America* 93(7), 1996, pp. 3043–7.

Kiecolt-Glaser, J. K., McGuire, L., Robles, T. F. and Glaser, R., 'Emotions, Morbidity, and Mortality: New Perspectives from Psychoneuroimmunology'. *Annual Review of Psychology* 53, 2002, pp. 83–107.

Lederbogen, F., Kirsch, P., Haddad, L. et al., 'City Living and Urban Upbringing Affect Neural Social Stress Processing in Humans'. *Nature* 474(7352), 2011, pp. 498–501.

Lee, Han-Joo, Cougle, Jesse R. and Telch, Michael J., 'Thought–Action Fusion and its Relationship to Schizotypy and OCD Symptoms'. *Behaviour Research and Therapy* 43(1), 2005, pp. 29–41.

Ogden, J., *Health Psychology: A Textbook*, 5th edn, Maidenhead: Open University Press/McGraw-Hill Education, 2012.

Pennebaker, J. W., 'Writing About Emotional Experiences as a Therapeutic Process'. *Psychological Science* 8(3), 1997, pp. 162–6.

Pennebaker, J. W. and Chung, C. K., 'Expressive Writing, Emotional Upheavals, and Health', in H. S. Friedman and R. C. Silver (eds), *Foundations of Health Psychology*, New York: Oxford University Press, 2007, pp. 263–84.

Pennebaker, J. W. and Seagal, J. D., 'Forming a Story: The Health Benefits of Narrative'. *Journal of Clinical Psychology* 55(10), 1999, pp. 1243–54.

Phillips, K. A., Coles, M. E., Menard, W. et al., 'Suicidal Ideation and Suicide Attempts in Body Dysmorphic Disorder'. *Journal of Clinical Psychiatry* 66(6), 2005, pp. 717–25.

Phillips, K. A. and Menard, W., 'Suicidality in Body Dysmorphic Disorder: A Prospective Study'. *American Journal of Psychiatry* 163(7), 2006, pp. 1280–2.

Rachman, S., *Anxiety*, 2nd edn, Hove: Psychology Press, 2004.

Schoenfeld, T. J., Rada, P., Pieruzzini, P. R., Hsueh, B. and Gould, E. P., 'Physical Exercise Prevents Stress-Induced Activation of Granule Neurons and Enhances Local Inhibitory Mechanisms in the Dentate Gyrus'. *The Journal of Neuroscience* 33(18), 2013, pp. 7770–7.

Streeter, C. C., Jensen, E., Perimutter, R. M., Cabral, H. J., Tian Hua, Terhun, D. B., Ciraulo, D. A., Renshaw, P. F., 'Yoga Asana Sessions Increase Brain GABA Levels: A Pilot Study'. *The Journal of Alternative and Complementary Medicine* 13(4), 2007, pp. 419–26.

Taylor, J., 'Is Technology Stealing Our (Self) Identities?' *Psychology Today*, online, 27 July 2011, <www.psychologytoday.com/print/70307>.

Taylor, S. E., Klein, L. C., Lewis, B. P., Gruenewald, T. A. et al., 'Biobehavioural Response to Stress in Females: Tend-and-Befriend, Not Fight-or-Flight'. *Psychological Review* 107(3), 2000, pp. 411–29.

Von Dawans, B., Fishbacher, U., Kirschbaum, C., Fehr, E. and Heinrichs, M., 'The Social Dimension of Stress Reactivity: Acute Stress Increases Prosocial Behavior in Humans'. *Psychological Science* 23(6), 2012, pp. 651–60.

Index

adrenaline 11, 16, 20, 23, 32
alcohol 17, 20, 30, 39, 83, 93
animal studies 7–8
anxiety
  anticipatory 77–8
  dental 52–4
  disorders 55–6
  illness and 16–17
  low blood sugar and 18
  medical conditions and 18
  mindset 90–2
  normal versus generalized 14
  and panic attacks 28–9
  parenting style and childhood
    anxiety 8–9
  performance 41–3
  physical symptoms of 23–4
  and stress 3–4
  taking responsibility for 1–3
  unlocking 7–8
  vision 32–3
  see also generalized anxiety
    disorder; panic; post-
    traumatic stress disorder;
    worry
assertion 96–102
  Bill of Assertive Rights 100
  When I say No, I Feel Guilty
    (Smith) 99
  why assertion matters 3
assertiveness techniques
  100–2
  Bill of Assertive Rights 100
  broken record 100–1
  Describe, Express, Specify,
    Consequences (DESC)
    101–2
  fogging 101
attachment 7, 26
avoidance 10, 14, 35, 53

blood pressure 17, 20, 31, 73–4, 77,
  82, 85
body dysmorphic disorder (BDD)
  36–7

Bowlby, John 7
brain
  amygdala 10, 21, 23, 92
  cortisol 16, 23, 27
  dopamine 19
  dynorphin 20–1
  endorphins 19–20
  glutamate and gamma-
    aminobutyric acid (GABA)
    18–19, 83–4, 87
  hippocampus 17, 19
  hypothalamic–pituitary–
    adrenocortical (HPA) system
    16–17
  oxytocin 26
  prefrontal cortex 8
  see also nervous system;
    self-help

Cannon, Walter 25
catastrophic thinking 6, 12
  see also worry
childhood 7–10, 66
city living 46–7
cognitive behavioural therapy
  (CBT) see therapy
context 1, 2, 9, 12–13, 21–2, 27,
  52, 72
Coplan, Jeremy 5
counselling see therapy
cultivating calm and confidence
  89–95
  memories and resentments
    89–90
cyberchondriasis 51
  see also technology

depression 4, 7–10, 19–21, 22,
  30, 37, 45, 52, 60, 67, 77, 81,
  87, 89
doctors 2–3, 56–7
Dweck, Carol S. 90–1

exercise 17, 95, 104
  effect on mood 19–20

exercise (*continued*)
    t'ai chi 20
    see also self-help
fears 13–14
    see also phobias; worry
fight or flight *see* stress
Freudenberger, Herbert J. 44
frozen trauma 66–7
    see also therapy

generalized anxiety disorder (GAD)
    5, 14–15, 21–2, 37, 55, 62

Hebb, Donald Olding 91
herbal remedies *see* self-help
HPA system *see* brain
hyperventilation *see* panic
hypervigilance *see* panic

immune system 17, 74, 77
inner conversations 41
irritable bowel syndrome (IBS)
    33–4
    self-help for 34

Liebowitz, Michael 9

medical conditions 17–18
memories 7, 10, 67, 73, 89
moving forwards 103–4

negative thinking 5, 6, 10–13, 36,
    41, 90
    neutralizing 11–13
    obsessional thinking 35–6
    superstitions 36
    thought–action fusion 36
nervous system 16–18, 20, 23–6,
    67, 73, 80, 83, 93
noradrenaline 16, 20

overbreathing *see* panic

pain 8, 19–21, 24, 33, 52–4, 74,
    77
panic 4, 13, 55, 79–80
    hyperventilation
        (overbreathing) 31–2
    hypervigilance 27–8

panic attacks 4, 13, 28–9
    see also self-help
Pennebaker, James W. 84
perfectionism 43–4
phobias 10, 14
    agoraphobia 30
    dental 53–4
    nomophobia 49
    social 37, 56
    specific 55
post-traumatic stress disorder
    (PTSD) 10, 28, 56

Schore, Allan 8
self-esteem 9–10, 54, 96
self-help 69–88
    breathing 71, 74–6
    confidence 80, 89, 90, 93,
        97–8
    diet 6, 17, 19, 33–4, 92–3,
        104
    exercise 34, 76, 84, 87–8
    herbal remedies 81–3
    increasing endorphins naturally
        20
    increasing GABA levels naturally
        19
    meditation 72, 76–8
    mindfulness 69–72, 90, 92, 95
    panic 4, 13–14, 28–32, 55, 75
    posture 71, 75, 78, 79–81
    problem-solving 62, 85–7
    relaxation 30, 38, 67, 72–8,
        81–2, 84, 95, 103
    resilience 5, 93–5
    sleep 30, 38–9, 82
    t'ai chi 30
    writing 84–5
    yoga 30, 83–4
sleep 4, 15, 20, 21, 22, 27, 34, 35,
    45, 104
social skills 9–10, 97
Spock, Benjamin 8
stress
    acute stress disorder 34–5
    anxiety and 3–4
    childhood stress and parenting
        8–9
    fight or flight 16, 20, 23–6, 32

MRI scanning, use of in
    comparing stress levels 46
tend-and-befriend 25–7
suicide 22, 37

Taylor, Jim 48
technology 47
    mobile devices 49–50
    role and nature in our lives
        48–9
    see also cyberchondriasis
therapy
    acceptance and commitment
        therapy 90
    cognitive behavioural therapy
        (CBT) 60–4
    counselling 64–6
    frozen trauma 66–7
    getting the best from 57–8

guided and supportive therapies
    59–68
hypnotherapy 67–8
SMART goals 62–3

Wells, Adrian 5
work and lifestyle 40–51
    burnout 44–5
    rust-out 45
worry
    catastrophic thinking 6
    chronic worrying 5–6
    link with high IQ 6
    mindset 90–2
    negative worrying 5–6
    positive worrying 6
    why we worry 3
    Worried Sick: Our Troubled Quest
        for Wellness (Barsky) 51